A JUST PEACE

A JUST PEACE

A Theological Exploration

Peter Matheson

Friendship Press · New York

1076

Originally published as *Profile of Love* by Christian
Journals Limited, Belfast, Northern Ireland.
Copyright © Christian Journals Limited 1979. This
edition, *A Just Peace,* published by Friendship Press,
Inc., New York 1981, by permission of the
originating house.

Editorial Offices: 475 Riverside Drive, New York,
NY 10115
Distribution Offiices: P.O. Box 37844, Cincinnati,
OH 45237

Printed in the United States of America

Introduction

"A Just Peace" sounds like a very high-flown document! But it isn't! It is an attempt to break through the wrinkled deadlock between pacifist and non-pacifist within the Church and beyond, and to find a new and relevant approach to the dire issues of war and justice in this decade. This Project arose out of the on-going discussions within the Church of Scotland, which in 1975 culminated in its General Assembly finding the Doctrine of the Just War no longer relevant to our modern situation. It appeared that many were happy to leave the matter there, feeling no urgency about filling the doctrinal void.

Whilst in some ways the doctrinal void must remain, we do believe that the work of this Project and this book will encourage new initiatives to relate the essential element of love as understood in the life and teaching of Jesus Christ, to personal life style as well as to national and international policies for a peaceful and just worldwide society. To this end the Fellowship of Reconciliation in Scotland has been glad to promote this study and to endorse this result.

The Project which Peter Matheson has carefully guided over the last two years attempts to come to a new stance and understanding by using the interaction of three study groups. The Edinburgh group's work was focussed on theological issues. In Belfast the group focussed particularly on the violent situation in Ireland with its roots in history, culture, and prejudice. The London group looked at the need for a life style which would not only make war outdated and unnecessary, but would also ensure sensitive justice for the populations living in towns, cities, and urban housing estates.

This study follows closely on the precedent set twenty years ago by Professor Josef L. Hromadka of the Evangelical Church of the Czech Brethern, with Dr. Johannes de Graaf of the International Fellowship of Reconciliation, in establishing as an essential element of the Christian Peace Conference the task of dialogue, focussed on the Christian approach to and understanding peace and justice. We hope this book will help to renew and further this dialogue.

Considerable thanks are due to the Joseph Rowntree Charitable Trust for the major funding of the Project and for additional help made available by the Radley Trust. The Trustees have encouraged the careful and unhurried work of the groups which provides the basis of these findings.

Peter Matheson himself has serviced the Project with great skill and insight, and though the actual text is his alone, the material made available to him through the groups has deepened and widened the scope of the whole debate. Having been a participant in the entire exercise myself, I can testify to the rigour and dedication of the men and women who faced up to the difficult issues and problems, both in the area of ideas, and in those of behaviour and policies. It appears to have been for us none other than an apocalyptic experience of seeing new truth emerge, unfettered by longstanding prejudice and arrogant pride. I hope this book helps each reader to share the same experience.

Ronald Beasley
Chairman
Fellowship of Reconcilation
in Scotland
July 1978.

Author's Note

This is not 'my book', although it appears under my name. Not only are whole chapters within it largely the work of other pens, the book is, in its entirety, the product of two years collective endeavour by some twenty people. In particular, without the encouragement of Ronald Beasley the project would never have got off the ground. I will be happy to take the credit if my editing has forged it into a coherent whole, but credit for any new ideas it has produced must go elsewhere.

Specifically, ch. 5 A Ground-Swell of Change owes much to Marcus Lefébure and Robert Murphy; ch. 6 Violence in Northern Ireland to the Belfast Group; ch. 7 The Just Revolution to Steven Mackie; ch. 8 Pointers Beyond Death to Elizabeth Templeton, *née* MacLaren; ch. 9 Life Style to Andrew Morton, Alex. Cosgrave, Alan Kreider and David Mumford; the other chapters originated with me. Obviously, however, none of the above are responsible for my formulation of their views.

None of us have any illusions about this being a definitive work. It is the deposit of a debate, and is meant to take the discussion about peace and justice a little further. The debate goes on.

Peter Matheson.

Peace Within Our Grasp

'It is not a matter of giving each man his due, but of giving each man everything, namely the absolute trust which leaves him room, prophetic room, to become a different man.' Roger Garaudy

Never before in his history has man presided over such an abundance of material resources and scientific expertise, such a plethora of international organisations, such a range of experience in peace-making operations. Peace is within our grasp today. All the presuppositions for it are there. Perhaps never before has the ordinary man and woman been able to express so evidently his yearning for peace. Think of the response across the world to the Peace People in love-torn Belfast. Think of the passion for peace in a city like Warsaw, every stone of whose old town has been rebuilt on the ashes of agony. Wherever children are cherished, wherever vulnerability has become the spur to love, there is a vested interest in peace with which no other interest under the face of heaven can even remotely begin to compare.

Our task is to harness this will to peace. To think big enough and to act imaginatively enough, to translate the dreams of the ordinary man into the realities of the politician. The multiple disasters which otherwise loom over us — nuclear war, population explosion, totalitarianism — spell out the consequences of failure. Our generation has to ensure that tomorrow's world will not just be a better one, but a qualitatively different one.

Peace *is* within our grasp, and our greatest stumbling-block lies not in the vested interests in war and violence — massive as they are — but in the soft-centredness of our own concept of peace. 'Just leave us in peace', is the instinctive reaction of most of us, most of the time, when disasters loom. We just want to be left alone, to be left 'in peace'. This is only human, and very often understandable.

The Christian analysis of reality, however, and the Christian hope offer us a potent antidote to this soft-centred concept of peace. They help us to see that peace is indivisible, that we, in our small and shrinking world, cannot buy our peace at the cost of the wretchedness of others. For the Bible peace and righteousness walk hand in hand. We will have to invite our neighbours in the Second World of Communism, and the Third World of the developing nations, and the Fourth World of urban deprivation in the West, to come together with us in the global village council and work out a *just peace*. We inhabit a grotesquely unjust world. Unless we redress its imbalances, peace will slip out of our grasp again.

The aim of this book is to tap the wealth of our Christian tradition as we face this imperative of peace. It may help us to develop a longer perspective and a richer battery of options. If we are to shake off the 'tyranny of actuality', to break out of the tired, old debates between pacifist and non-pacifist, to forge new solutions for the unprecedented opportunities before us, then we must broaden the canvas of the current debate about war, peace, and justice. Analysing, moralising, prophesying is not enough.

14

Over a period of two years a study project initiated by the Fellowship of Reconciliation in Scotland and financed by the Rowntree Trust has sought to break new ground in this way, to explore what resources the Christian tradition has to offer to resolve the age-old tension between our yearning for peace and the claims of human rights and social justice.

Three groups, ecumenical in composition and with an approximately equal number of pacifists and non-pacifists, began meeting in the autumn of 1975. One, in Belfast, concentrated on peace and justice in Northern Ireland, one in London on the question of a non-violent life-style, while the third group, in Edinburgh, addressed itself more to the theological issues.

In their monthly meetings these groups attempted to relate our contemporary dilemmas about war and violence to their roots in the past. They probed the way in which certain basic theological concepts, such as original sin, have influenced the Churches' attitudes to war and peace, violence and non-violence. The Church's history was scrutinised in the light of contemporary experience, and a fascinating, if sometimes difficult, interaction developed between past theology and present practice. All three groups kept in close touch with one another, seeking to collate experience and pool perspectives. My own role was to produce the historical papers and to co-ordinate the whole.

This book is the result. It preaches a quiet revolution, away from a privileged Church to a Church of the people, away from a quietist piety to a spirit-uality of achievement, away from an academic

15

understanding of faith to a committed confessionalism. You will, I think, be startled how much common ground emerges in the process between pacifist and non-pacifist. I hope you will also agree that this is theology 'with its feet on the ground', nourished by reality. If not, the fault does not lie with the participants of the three groups. Throughout our two years of meeting the disciplines of realism were constant. Nearly all comments related to personal experience.

In fact, group members had first-hand experience of gang warfare in Britain, of 'the Troubles' in Northern Ireland, of revolution in Africa, of communal warfare in India. They never allowed the theorisers among us to get away with anything, at least not for long!

This book, then, is through and through a corporate effort. Such insights as it may have are those of all the project members, and its indebtedness to them is total, though, quite obviously, responsibility for this final form must be my own. I hope that the book will not only convey the substance of the discussions, but something of their flavour.

They were very personal. Listening was careful. There was no jockeying for the chance to get one's own point in. Few of us can have experienced groups which were so unplagued by preconceived views and prejudice, though robust differences of opinion often emerged. We included, after all, academics and 'practitioners', laymen and clerics, Catholics and Protestants, in our numbers. Humour was frequent, but at times we were all deeply moved. These were, then, no academic talk-shops, but an intimate and informal sharing of faith, doubt and experience. Hopefully something of this will 'come over'.

The eventual course of the project was never predictable, as each group was deliberately chosen to represent a wide spectrum of views and was encouraged to produce its own papers and develop its own style of working. At times we despaired of anything coherent emerging at all, despite, or perhaps because of the frankness which characterised all the discussions. At the end of the day, however, we hope that we have been able to produce a fresh, human, and reasonably coherent contribution to the current debate.

A word or two about the origins of the project may be in order. They are nothing if not down to earth, for they have to do with the annual deliberations of the Church and Nation Committee at the Church of Scotland's General Assembly. Year after year there has been a set-piece confrontation between a pacifist minority and a non-pacifist majority on the just war issue. This has assumed different forms, sometimes concentrating, for example, on nuclear war. The outcome, however, in terms of voting, has been highly predictable. It is doubtful if either party, for all the rhetoric about 'agonising decisions', has access to the mind or heart of the other. The debate has run into the sands. It has become a cultic occasion of decidedly limited interest; of none at all to the 'world outside'.

One suspects that there must be countless other examples within the Churches of an impasse like this. The issue of the just war may well be an important one, but to the majority of people, responsible and concerned people within the Churches, this is not self-evident. Hence the cultic character of the confrontation. One cannot expect a hurtful re-consideration of long-loved clichés when the issue appears abstract and academic, and both the just war theory and the pacifist alternative appear to many in just this utopian light.

If, however, the question of war impinges very indirectly on people's consciousness the same cannot be said about violence. Anxiety about violence and fascination by it are very prevalent in our society today. We are uneasily aware of vast reservoirs of pent-up aggressions within ourselves and within our social, national and international orders. To dam them with the traditional moral and religious sanctions appear increasingly inadequate. At the same time, the socially acceptable outlets for releasing aggression have been dramatically restricted. In Britain, at least, concription has disappeared. It is no longer the done thing to duck the witch, or string up the gypsy, or lynch the Jew. 'Pak-bashing' is frowned on; racialism offends the liberal conscience. We are short, in a word, on scapegoats.

What, then, do we do about a violence which the very merits of our society has made it more difficult to dam or divert? What do we do about the violence within ourselves, our families, our work-relationships? Is political involvement the answer, or social, or educational, or what? What, if anything, do the Churches as social groupings contribute to the resolution of such conflicts? How do we rate personally as reconcilers? Does our traditional life-style, e.g. the emphasis on the indissolubility of marriage, imply a commitment to reconciliation *at all costs*? Is the task of the Church to maximise happiness in an

18

unjust world, or to encourage the exploited to rebel against their apparent 'fate'?

The national problems point to the international ones, too. For who are the 'exploited' today? The answer of the Third World is explicit enough, and itself explains the fact that the contemporary Christian conscience is more concerned with revolution than with war, with the just peace than the just war. The Christian in the West has barely begun to wrestle with these new verities, and clearly has much more listening ahead of him in the years to come.

This particular project originates from the concern of the Fellowship of Reconciliation in Scotland to encourage listening and reflection on this dual front, domestic and international. It is by no means clear at this stage what, if any, connection there is between the two, apart from the fact that both involve violence and both concern us. The first, violence within Britain, is apparently apolitical, non-ideological, anarchic or even criminal, the second is eminently political, frequently ideological, and only branded as criminal by those with an obvious stake in the status quo. The New Left, of course, attempted to relate the two but its diagnosis has, for bad as well as good reasons, found little favour of late. A more immediate connection for us is found in Northern Ireland. As a problem it is domestic enough. We should probably talk of the British problem, not the Irish one, for Westminster created it. Yet its international ramifications are obvious. Its political and ideological (Christian!) components are not far to seek; nor are its anarchic and criminal ones. At no stage will we be able to talk of peace, justice or revolution without thinking of, and with,

Northern Ireland.

As far as Great Britain at least is concerned, we face such issues in a mood of shocked sobriety, if not of depression or even alarm. Successive blows to our self-esteem have left us badly winded. The retreat from Imperial power to a segment of Europe has turned into a rout. Problems of identity abound as we seek to adjust to the changed realities. Can we who once presumed to 'civilize' half the globe even manage to put our own house in order? Communal and sectarian violence are one side of the coin, cynicism and a low level of political consciousness the other. We just want to be left alone, to be left 'in peace'.

This very superficial understanding of peace is paralleled by a notable disenchantment with the idea of justice. In few ages can the Puritans have been so out of fashion as in our own, and the concern for justice appears a disquietingly 'Puritan' one. Why should we lacerate ourselves about problems so vast and complex that they cannot in any case be solved? In our far from confident culture the sheer volume of information provided by the media produces a form of inverted conscientisation, mesmerising the individual into weary acquiescence. Commitment itself has become a dirty word.

The same loss of orientation is evident on the theological level. Barthianism has not long survived the demise of Liberalism, and *its* successors in turn have suffered almost instant obsolescence: Bultmann's demythologizing programme, Secular theology, Death of God theology, Process theology etc etc. With rare unanimity radical and conservative Christians are agreeing to bypass theology. In the current

20

literature of the World Council of Churches, for example, it is hard to shake off the impression that theology's function is simply to provide slogans for programmes (development, justice, peace etc.) whose rationale is found elsewhere.

Yet there are clear advantages to this 'loss of bearings', politically and theologically. It makes possible, as never before, a searching critique of the way in which the Church's teachings in the past have actually functioned *politically*. Here the Third World and the Church in Eastern Europe have the word. The main contribution of the Churches in the West may well be a willingness to re-scrutinise its own theological tradition in the light of such criticism.

Another advantage is the impatience with theological jargon of all varieties. If there is any way through to a new theological language it will only be through the pain of intellectual and emotional rigour with ourselves and with others. Any credible theology must begin with our past failures, our present injustices, and the future we have denied to our neighbour's children.

Thirdly, ecclesiastical triumphalism is at a decided discount, at least outside the charmed circles of the Establishment. We harbour few illusions about the impact of theology or the Church on the world. We are not at all sure whether we want a 'Christianised' world at all. Our problem with theology is that orthodox theology and churchmanship have themselves done so much to bolster up injustice. So often it has been the 'heretics' and the schismatics who have developed a theology of conscience, in the teeth of the Magisterial Church's resistance. The

21

social conscience of a Church has tended to be in inverse ratio to the 'orthodoxy' of its theology.

If this is so, then we must be very clear what we are doing in trying to sketch a theology of the just peace. What is the criterion for what? Is a just peace defined as one which is well-grounded theologically? Or is a 'good' theology one which gives effectual sanction to a world order in which oppressed peoples gain a better deal?

The conviction behind this project is that this alternative is falsely put. We certainly have to lay the ghosts of the past. Where theology has become absolutised and ideologised we have to discard it, like the image-breakers of Byzantium and the Reformation who could not see the ultimate for the penultimate. Where the Church makes a living by selling nostalgia it should be treated as Luther treated the indulgence sellers. We have to be aware of how unbelievably anti-modern the past is, how unbridgeable the chasm between the then and the now; we have to shrug off the burden of tradition.

Yet this very impatience with the past can itself become an idolatry. The concern to narrow the range of problems to be faced, and the questions to be asked, to the realm of politics or economics or technology may be understandable, but it could not be more misplaced. The arrogant and ignorant rejection of the past in fact forecloses the future, condemns it in advance to follow the hunched vision of our present era. It is precisely the alien nature of our tradition, its 'unrealised possibilities' which are the corrective, the sense of perspective which we need. For the future the present needs the past.

A theology of the just peace can only emerge

from a creative interaction between the moral imperatives which we experience vividly and immediately, for example, the call to solidarity with the helpless and oppressed, and a doctrinal tradition about which we are much less certain.

It will not do to dissemble, to keep quiet about our hesitations and doubts on the faith side of the equation in order to 'get on with the job', to push through necessary reforms and initiatives, for this appears very like 'using' the institutions of the Church for socio-political ends.

Nor, in my view, though there may well be disagreement here, is it a matter of accepting new ethical insights but blandly welding them to the 'unchanging' doctrines of the faith. Part, one suspects, of the problem of much World Council of Churches literature is that it tends to do just this. The new wine is poured into the old wine-skins of Western Christendom, a programme of socio-political progress is uneasily yoked to a backward-looking faith.

What may be emerging is a new understanding of the faith commitment of the Christian. There have been, our Christian past reminds us, Christian martyrs, men and women ready to die for what they confessed. What, if anything, could we conceive ourselves dying for today? Not, one imagines, for the doctrines of the Trinity. What transcends our desire to stay alive? In less melodramatic terms, by what largely unspoken creed do we *actually* live?

Are we as bankrupt theologically as in some moods we like to pretend? Or are our faculties perhaps fogged by the very plethora of resources and perspectives at our disposal? Have we to begin looking at the actual sources of our positive convictions, at what makes us do what we do and be what we are? Ever since Bonhoeffer we have been fumbling towards a theological reinterpretation of apparently secular concerns. It may be that this project will nudge us further in this direction.

For implicit in social and political commitment is an awareness of transcendence. Why do we recognise the just claim of the exploited, even when it conflicts with our self-interest? Why this quite extraordinary modern phenomenon of daily, conscientious attention to the news, allowing the accumulated agonies of the whole world to seep into our living-room? Why do we tolerate a brand of drama, music, film, novel, art infinitely more demanding in their realism than at any previous time in our history? It is here that we feel the finger of God upon us: in this solidarity with the oppressed, in this investment of current affairs with eschatological significance, in this sensitivity to language and symbol. None of these are virtues we can crow about. They are recognition markers of a transcendent claim on our being and living.

We live in a world where the pressures in favour of violence are strong, seductive and inescapable. What we need is a doctrine to account for the depth of these pressures and to show the possibilities of countering them. We need a theology of the just peace.

The difficulty is that peace, generally understood as 'not being at war', tends to have a negative ring. It sounds like a validation for the status quo, a prescription for apathy. Yet as .a look around any housing estate in contemporary Britain will show, apathy is the soul-sister to violence, bred in and by the same dehumanising environment. Today's glue-sniffer or TV addict, defensively switching off the life-support system, is tomorrow's recruit for the National Front. A concept of peace must be yoked to the more dynamic thrust of justice, with its concern for relationships and human dignity, if it is counter such apathy.

Peace is within our grasp if we can develop this sense of solidarity with the oppressed, not as a moral duty (God forbid), but because we recognise a transcendent claim on our being and living. The naked, battered body of Steve Biko, bumping its way to death in the back of a South African police van, becomes invested with eschatological significance. Is this what Revelation is to us? If so, how does it relate to Scripture, tradition, piety? Are the latter only of historical interest, pointers to what should be *our* doctrines, or are they normative? Do we use, for example, Biblical norms to sift the news for what is significant? Finally, what do we understand by the lordship of Christ? Is He more than founder and teacher? May it be that we only find out as we put ourselves alongside the outsider as he did?

All these trends towards a new understanding of faith will be meaningless unless progress is simultaneously made towards evolving a different *life-style*. Declamations about solidarity with the oppressed remain mere rhetoric until accompanied by a substantial, lived-out reality, and this, of course, has ecclesiastical as well as personal implications. The new humanity has to be bodied out in our being as well as our talking.

The pit-falls here are all too numerous. The aim

must be a new freedom, not a new rigorism, and a freedom from role-playing and status-seeking and insecurity as well as from overt materialism. It is fairly evident that the individual can only make limited progress on his own. He needs, she needs support. Communal living may be utopian for the majority, but this need not be an alibi for evading determined and imaginative initiatives in the pooling of resources, for example. It is not a matter of using life-style as an index of one's own, or still worse of others' sincerity, but of seeking to humanise all our relationships, of living 'without the mask'. There is probably no greater obstacle to our credibility as peace-makers than the facade of friendliness we present to the world.

Conclusions.
(At the end of each chapter a few conclusions will be added. Their purpose is to summarise the argument and provide a convenient peg for group discussion.)

1. A more positive concept of peace is required, as at present 'peace' is devalued in political and theological discussion.
2. Peace, whether at home or abroad, is only a legitimate aim if linked to the pursuit of justice.
3. In the past the Christian Church has frequently sanctioned an unjust status quo by a one-sided emphasis on reconciliation.

The Powers That Be

'Society is the product of our wants and government of our wickedness.' Thomas Paine.

'The decisive factor: The Church on the defensive. No taking risks for others.' Dietrich Bonhoeffer.

The mark of the traditional pacifist has been that of conscientious objection. His individual conscience set limits to the demands of the state. He contracted out. This rejection of the coercive jurisdiction of the state led occasionally to attempts to form a new, non-violent society. On the whole, however, the suspicion with which the pacifist viewed all exercise of political power led to a separation or withdrawal from the political realm. At best a sub-culture or counter-culture emerged, often in uneasy tension with the authorities. The pacifist offered a critique of political power but, apparently, no realistic alternative.

The extraordinary feature of contemporary Christian radicalism, on the other hand, is its optimism about the possibility of a just society. This is particularly true of Christians in the developing countries. What Lenin once hoped from the Soviets plus electricity, the so-called Third World now expects from conscientisation plus technology. The humanising of politics, it is believed, and the politicising of economics can face, tackle, and solve the problems of hunger, disease, illiteracy and deprivation. This qualitatively better, juster world is the justification for revolutionary change, the revolution for human dignity.

Before we take up the question of revolutionary violence, which too often has monopolised Western attention, we must come to terms with this fundamental revaluation of the political realm as such. Going far beyond Christian Socialism, it represents a quite new phenomenon in Christian history: a concern not just to mould or control society but to transform it. Evil can be crushed underfoot, the potentialities of human existence unpackaged, and all this on a world-wide basis. For 'space-ship earth' has entered the era of universal history. The whole family of nations *must and can be changed*. The extremities of need clutch desperately at the promises of development.

These promises, as we all know, have proved a mockery. Development has signally failed to deliver. As the gap between rich and poor nations widens, the prospects of a largely technocratic solution — never very high — fade away completely. We still have some time to manoeuvre, we in the West, for militarily and economically the 'threat' from the under-privileged is still minimal, and we could, no doubt, butcher any uprising as the princes and bishops butchered the peasants as modern Europe was born. Flickerings of hope from the United Nations even suggest that genuine dialogue between rich and poor has not yet totally broken down. What is sure is the surge of the discontented throughout the world to politics, on a scale dwarfing that of the French and Russian revolutions. In such a context pacifist agonising over one's individual conscience must appear irrelevant, if not egoistic.

This process is, of course, largely a secular one. It is a matter of prudence and honesty for the Western (or Northern) Christian to recognise that his first and perhaps lasting reaction to the whole process is one of apprehension. We have our own experience with revolutions, and know how they devour their children. We have as yet no experience of a revolution directed primarily against us. We can, however, imagine at least some of its consequences. The least we can do is confess our anxieties.

It is, for example, very probable that much trendy enthusiasm for revolution in the developed countries is as motivated by anxiety as any Colonel Blimp reactions. One already notes signs of an expedient accommodation to revolutionary vocabulary in the most unexpected ecclesiastical quarters. There is no doubt the hope that a theological baptism of revolution will produce a tame breed of Christian revolutionaries with whom a 'sensible compromise' will be possible. All this is as predictable as it is unrealistic. More will be demanded of us than gestures.

But there are religious dimensions to this secular process. Ironically, as Hannah Arendt points out, no one needs divine authority so much as the revolutionary. The status quo has the authority of tradition; it sails under the flag of inertia. Innovation, however, has to be justified and in times such as ours the appearance of a theology of revolution is inevitable. A new frame-work of values is required, a changed pattern of legitimacy. It is worth remembering, however, that the National Socialist revolution also produced its own brand of theological reflection, one tailored to its 'revolution'.

Misunderstanding at this point would be unfortunate. One is not arguing against a theology of revolution as such, but against too glib an assumption that we can read off theology from the expectant eyes of the oppressed. The human response to personal humiliation can be as uncreative as the response to affluence. Morally there is little to choose from between rage and indifference. The temptation to forget this is, perhaps, particularly strong where guilt-obsessed Westerners seek to develop a theology of revolution on *behalf* of the oppressed. All manner of confusions then become operative, not least a novel form of paternalism.

The contribution of the West might well be a more modest one. To assist this profound re-evaluation of the political role of Christians in the 'Third World' it could offer its own centuries-long experience of Church-State relationships, not of course in any sense as a model to be followed, but as a whole series of models worthy of reflection. The resultant dialogue might help to clarify the very different implications of a theology of revolution for Christians in developed and developing countries. We must, for example, take care that a moralising concern for a just peace does not totally uproot the Western Christian from his cultural nexus. Northern Ireland might well have some lessons to give in this regard. Man, when deprived of his sense of identity, is the most dangerous of animals.

What, then, has the Christian tradition to say about the 'powers that be', about the theological basis of legitimate authority?

It is the New Testament, heart-rock of the Christian faith, which immediately has us stumbling and gasping for breath. The Old Testament with its prophetic witness chimes in with much that we would want to say today. Even the dour verities of the historical books help one to chop away at cant and hypocrisy. But what can we make of 'render to Caesar', 'be submissive to the powers that be', when the unambiguous exegesis given these texts by century after century of Church history is that of deference to authority, passivity under authoritarian regimes, and above all the curious spectacle of Christian armies marching out to slaughter one another, secure in the knowledge that both God and Caesar are getting their due. What wonder that the credibility of the Christian political ethic is nil? The German Christians, who almost to a man bowed their heads under the National Socialist storm, witness to the total bankruptcy of this tradition. If that does not choke us to speechlessness nothing will.

Let us be quite clear about this. Only the blindest and most ignorant chauvinist can doubt that the German Christian in the Third Reich experienced moral qualms, frequently moral outrage. But it was the *Bible* which tied his hands, the Christian political tradition which prevented his outrage being translated into action. It was simply unthinkable to resist the authorities. It was sinful. It was contrary to the will of God.

Thus those Germans who stood by while the Jews were hustled away in the furniture vans represent all Western Christendom. The futility of their balled fists is ours too. Without in any way playing down the staggering difficulties of any effective political witness in such a crazed and totalitarian situation, one still has to pose the bleak question: What is a faith worth which fails so pathetically? What price Christianity after *this* witness?

It is, of course, significant that the Copernican

31

turn in Christian political thinking after the War came from the Third World, which is free from such guilt burdens. In the West the old patterns of thought still have a remarkable hold, Dresden, Algeria and Vietnam notwithstanding. Only the Churches of Eastern Europe have had to review their stance fundamentally, a difficult and costly procedure by no means concluded yet. In the enormous shake-up in our political thinking, then, the developed countries of the West, burdened by the weight of their tradition, lag *badly* behind.

Enough has perhaps been said to demonstrate that a tossing around of Biblical texts will not suffice. We will have to come back to the Biblical texts, of course, but the substantial commentary on them must be the actual influence of Church and theology on the political evolution of Europe. It is this we must now review.

It is, first of all, impossible to overlook the *quietist* element in the Christian tradition. The first Christians were certainly not revolutionaries, in any normal sense of the word. Politically they were unexciting and unexcited. Christ order and world order did not seem to touch one another, at least as far as political involvement was concerned. They produced no new political theories or initiatives. They offered no frontal challenge to the structures of power or the patterns of society. They do not seem to have been interested in changing society. Indeed the exhortation to obey the authorities as the instruments of God's justice implies that for them the *pax Romana* was already a just one.

The just peace, then, was already in existence. Their eyes were fixed on an eschatological horizon, on the new age that was imminent, which would sweep aside all human institutions as Christ himself came to rule. It is impermissible to read off today's concerns for secular justice, democracy, power-sharing, welfare state etc. from this type of perspective.

But why did Paul lay such emphasis on submission: of women to men, of the Christian to the authorities? Can everything be explained by the eschatological emphasis? Did he simply reflect here the conventional wisdom of his time? The Roman Empire, after all, was not a democracy, so there was no possibility of peaceful change. Or does his approach betray a positive recognition of the socio-political achievements of Rome which deserves to be taken more seriously than has often been the case? At least he does not fall into an easy dualism of the sectarian variety, more than can be said of some of the more hot-headed of the Christian martyrs. They certainly tended to daemonise the state, and thus to provoke one of the most religiously tolerant of Empires to persecute them.

Sociologically, the primitive Church was in any case a tiny, insignificant grouping. In the nature of things one would not expect this huddle of the under-privileged to develop much in the way of political initiatives. Marxist categories seem singularly unhelpful here. Neither as property-owners nor as those with social status did they seem to have any particular interest in supporting the status quo. Yet they did want to see anarchy avoided, and crime punished. They had no incentive to see the establishment overturned; it was preferable to the Zealots or still more unknown quantities. In some rather impersonal sense they approved of the Empire as the custodian of justice, a justice understood as 'law and order' rather than in prophetic terms. Rome afforded the Church both peace and stability and a degree of protection against Judaism. The most interesting question is perhaps why there was so little of the Old Testament prophetic tradition in the early church, despite Jesus being seen as continuing the prophetic line. Not the least of the problems of the contemporary Christian pacifist is that the undoubted pacifism of the Early Church was set within this quietistic framework.

As the Empire was 'Christianised' the quietist role fell increasingly to the 'heretic', schismatic and Jew, but it never completely disappeared. The great monastic movement was a form of quietism, in origin at least. Lutheranism had strong quietist tendencies, especially in its Pietist form; the same is true of Eastern Orthodoxy, and nearly all mystical movements. One need hardly mention the quietist Jesus of the charismatics of our own day. It is by no means to be confused with resignation or indifferentism, although it can slide into this, and is often accompanied by a dynamic church life is nonpolitical respects. Much traditional pacifism has been of this variety.

At the other pole to quietism, and historically often preceding or following it, is the *assimilationist* model, sometimes in theocratic, sometimes in Erastian form. We have an example of this close integration of Church and society very early in the Church's history, when under Constantine and Theodosius Christianity developed into the state religion in the fourth century.

Hailed as a divine miracle by the triumphalist prose of the church historian Eusebius, it certainly was a quite startling reversal of roles. No one who reads the accounts of the early Christian martyrs, even in our blasé age, can fail to be moved by their tenacity, courage, and above all serenity. Yet this martyr church, apparently so radiant in its confidence, collapsed into the arms of the state when Constantine discovered Christ as the superior war god. With scarcely a scruple the Church gratefully accepted its new status, its new freedom, wealth, privileges, and opportunities. With considerable élan it set about using the coercive power of the Empire to enforce uniformity of doctrine and church order, even to exclude non-Christians from the army.(!)

The achievements were, in fact, considerable. Churchmen like Ambrose of Milan never engaged in uncritical adulation of what was, in any case, a hard-pressed Empire, and exercised the right to prophetic criticism on frequent occasions. The legal code was humanised; church art and architecture flourished; missionary and pastoral opportunities were exploited. Unless, with the Anabaptists, one holds that the true Church *must* be a minority cause, it would seem the sheerest romanticism to condemn this new phase as the Fall of the Church. We cannot, in any case, unwrite history. It happened.

That it happened, however, and how it happened, is highly significant. In the first place, it prompts us to caution as regards the martyrdom period. Curiously it is the assimilationist, the establishment type, who is particularly prone to use this period as a selling-point for Christianity, to stress the heroic superiority of the faith to all dangers. Yet the indecent speed of the Church's capitulation to Constantine would seem to indicate almost the opposite: a weariness of taut nerves and anxious minds, a yearning for divine intervention which enabled Constantine's military successes to be accepted as God-given. This overwhelming sense of relief is a highly understandable human reaction. It is not, however, the received picture of martyrdom as the seed of the Church. The Church flourished when it thankfully turned its back on martyrdom except as a pious memory. Suffering was clearly not the high road to success for the Church, as many Church accounts have tended to imply.

Secondly, given the fact that the Church could no longer be the counter-culture, how creatively did it use the chance to develop new political and social initiatives? If the programme of the Christianisation of the Empire meant that world order and Christ's order were to be assimilated to one another what did this mean in practice? The clericalisation and institutionalisation of the Church did not, of course, begin with Constantine, but how far was the new State Church simply using its new prestige and power to further this process? One notes, for example, the embittering effect of using political power to settle doctrinal controversies and disputes about Church order; the fostering of hierarchical rather than pastoral attitudes; the enhanced social status of the episcopate; the condescending attitude, especially in the Eastern Empire, to the 'barbarian' Christian, and the ominous strengthening of juridical tendencies within the Church.

Unquestionably this assimilationist model was to

remain the normative pattern for both the Western and the Eastern Church until the successive Revolutions of the last two centuries tore it to shreds. What we tend to forget today is its honest idealism, when it undergirded loyalty to Emperor (or later King and country) with religious motifs, and defended the True Faith with the secular arm. They were conceived as belonging together. The surviving mummery associated with coronation oaths and the like should not blind us to the fundamental conviction behind the stress on the Christian's dual loyalty to Church and State: that of the secular implications of the Christian faith. First Papalism, and then Nationalism may have distorted the face of Christendom and prevented the *pax Romana* becoming the *pax Christiana* in any very satisfactory form, but the dream of Christendom had its dignity, and we do well to recognise the good conscience of those who pursued it.

Sometimes hard to distinguish from the assimilationist pattern, but in fact carrying a quite different ethos is what we might dub the *concordat model*. This is quite simply a marriage of convenience, often a quite expedient or cynical one between Church and State. Obvious examples are the various compacts made by the Papacy with the emerging monarchies of France, England, Spain in order to defeat the power-sharing proclivities of Conciliarism in the 15th century. Papal monarchy and secular monarchies found a common interest in suppressing such constitutionalist tendencies. A hard bargain was struck in which the secular powers withdrew support for Conciliarism in exchange for a more or less free hand in administering the churches within their territories.

Countless examples of such bizarre coalitions are to be found in the seventeenth century, in the era of confessionalism and religious war. The bigot is seldom fastidious about the means he uses to achieve his sacred end. The ludicrous attempts of the Scottish Covenanters to impose Presbyterianism on England by selling their military strength first to hesitant Parliament and then to Charles II are a case in point. Roman Catholicism today is still trying to live down its ugly concordats with Fascism in Germany, Italy, and Spain. The end-result, of course, of all such concordats is to weaken the credibility and the authority of both partners.

On the other hand, even here the picture is not altogether black. The juridical tendencies within the Church which they reflect often proved a fair way of incorporating and representing and reconciling conflicting interests. The canon lawyer, with his compacts and contracts and accommodations, based on a firm sense of realism and often on equity, may have been the unwitting forerunner of that most remarkable of European innovations, the convention, Diet, Parliament: the representative institution, unknown to all other cultures, on which so much of our European democratic tradition rests.

The frank recognition of self-interest and conflict of interest may in the long run prove a more stable basis for political authority than the detached obedience of the quietist or the enthusiastic loyalty of the assimilationist.

This brings us to our final model, which we can call the *puritan* or rigorist one. In its Calvinist form, it has been particularly influential in our Anglo-

Saxon history. It is, however, far from being an exclusively Protestant pattern, and significantly the Jesuits, the most resolute foes of the Calvinists, had a very similar outlook.

It is now generally accepted that there is no direct line of causation between, say, Calvinism and capitalism, still less democracy. Evidence accumulates, however, that there are all manner of interesting indirect links. Calvinists and Jesuits, because of the firmness of their confessional stance, were simply not willing to compromise themselves in a diaspora situation, when they were in exile or in the minority. In an age when everyone was expected to toe the religious line laid down by their ruler, they refused to do so. The fact that the ruler enjoyed a flawless pedigree made no impression on them, nor the fact that he or she was their anointed and, by implication, God-approved ruler. The theory of the Divine Right of Kings, with its Platonic assumption about the derivation of power from above, left them cold.

Political authority, in their view, had to validate itself by functioning effectively. The ruler had duties as well as rights, and when he failed to carry out these duties by governing according to God's will his authority was forfeit. The contractualist implications here were already evident in the Conciliarist critique of *papal* absolutism in the fifteenth century and no doubt rest ultimately on Aristotelian assumptions about the nature of political power. The strength, however, of the Calvinist case was the conscientious belief that in Scripture they possessed the most accurate of plumb lines for the guidance of errant monarchs. From this, too, they derived a pattern of church government and discipline which constituted virtually a state within the state. It is thus one of the ironies of history that the most intolerant proponents of confessionalism, the Calvinists and Jesuits, did more than anyone else to foster the growth of pluralist beliefs and institutions. Where they were too strong to be suppressed, yet not strong enough to impose their will on everyone else, they proved one of the most effective brakes on absolutism. The infra-structure they created, consecrated to the greater glory of God, proved mightily productive to Mammon, and a fertile ground for the dynamics of modernisation. Where, on the other hand, they gained a clear ascendancy, as in Spain or, for a time, in Scotland, the dead hand of orthodoxy inhibited progress and a new form of caesaro-papalism emerged.

The execution of Charles I illustrates the strengths and weaknesses of this puritan approach. With the invaluable help of the Common Law tradition, the functionalist critique triumphed. Political authority was desacralised, depersonalised, demytholigised. Religion refused to be used as a rubber-stamp to legitimise the 'powers that be'. The revolutionary potential of the Christian faith was revealed.

On the other hand, the Commonwealth did not last. It proved unequal to the appallingly difficult task of creating a new focus of loyalty, a sense of identity, an alternative web of social relationships. The godly, it seems, seldom make good politicians. The zealot may create a New Model army, but he lacks the patience and the pragmatism for consensus politics. This most religiously motivated of revolutions foundered for all manner of reasons, not least the class tensions within its own ranks, but perhaps its very virtues brought it down. Those who embark on the course of revolution, who slice with their scalpel into that most delicate and sensitive of organisms, human society, need not only nerve, skill and vision — for men like Cromwell had all of that — they need cold ruthlessness, a readiness to sweep aside anything that stands in the way of the cause. A revolution transforms the political landscape overnight, but the people who rub their bleary eyes the next morning are the same people who were there the day before. Their values cannot change overnight; their stake was in the society that disappeared in the whirlwind. What is to be done with them until they see the 'error' of their previous ways? The techniques of conscientisation may help to humanise the revolution today. One hopes so.

The revolutionary pattern itself, of course, has only emerged in the most recent of years as a Christian possibility. The French, American, and Russian Revolutions were secular, if not anti-clerical and anti-religious phenomena. Perhaps the most momentous of all, the Chinese, is far too close to us for any sort of perspective to be possible, but even the most enthusiastic of Christian apologists will find difficulty in claiming it as a step-child of Christianity.

The truth is, and we have to face it, that the restructuring of our entire social and political fabric in the last two centuries brought about by this succession of revolutions owes virtually nothing to the Christian Churches, with the partial exception of the American Revolution. Indeed, the Churches fought them, with few exceptions, every inch of the way: the Holy Alliance mentality of Catholicism, the 'throne and altar' synthesis of a National Protestantism, the 'holy Russia' myth of Orthodoxy. Holiness was as synonymous with political reaction as authoritarian attitudes with Christian values. Those who cast scorn today on Liberalism and Modernism might reflect that they were one of the very few exceptions to this rule, and even they, of course, had no time for social revolution.

Let us try to summarise. Crucial to any theology of a just peace is an understanding of political authority. Many if not most of the presuppositions of modern political thinking, and certainly of those concerned for revolutionary change, are derived not from the Christian tradition at all, but from the great revolutions of the last two centuries. We are not democrats because we are Christians. Our democratic, and egalitarian values are borrowed from other sources. There is a long and honourable Christian tradition for such clothes-pinching, and we need not be ashamed of it. We should, however, be aware of it.

The question now arises whether, in pursuit of the just peace, we also feel contrained and justified in pinching revolutionary garments. If so have we a creative contribution of our own to make?

The time is certainly ripe for new thinking and new initiatives. Democracy in contemporary Britain is very much under fire. In Northern Ireland, for example, democracy appears to mean rule of a Catholic minority by a Protestant majority and has, to all intents and purposes, broken down. Within Britain as a whole the ten per cent of the population suffering from multiple deprivation, our 'Fourth World', is effectively disenfranchised and likely to remain so. A 'democratic' majority will always be against them. There is also the broader danger of a retreat into 'privatism', a disenchantment with all political engagement, stemming from the low level of leadership in national politics. Indeed many suggest that in Britain today we are passing through a period of 'cultural homelessness'. The nationalist movements in Scotland, Wales and Northern Ireland and the parallel phenomenon of 'little Englandism' may well reflect this feeling of home-lessness, a loosening of old bonds, a quest for a new identity.

Grunwick, on the one hand, and the National Front, on the other, signalise the danger that this sense of being uprooted will be exploited by poli-tical extremists. But the opportunities are also formidable, for this exodus from traditional ways may be a necessary staging-house on the journey to a more just society. The Christian has the advantage of a base, a society of committed friends, which provides support and discipline and enables action to be taken. With such an identifying community behind him (the image of Mother Church) he or she can take the risks involved. What all this means is that the blanket advocacy of obedience to the 'powers that be' offers no kind of guide to fruitful action, to the task of cashing out in specific political terms the implications of 'love your neighbour'. In Northern Ireland, for example, traditional Christian theorising about the state and the forms of govern-ment seems quite irrelevant. Whatever may be said in principle about authority being God-given, in practice the abuse of authority over decades by a Protestant majority is the issue which has still to be faced.

There is a new questioning, and not only in Northern Ireland, of the Christian commitment to 'democracy', if by the latter is meant majority or consensus politics. In its inception, at least, Christianity was a *minority* cause. Should the loyalty of the Christian be to the political middle ground or is his solidarity not rather with the under-privileged, nationally and internationally? Was it not their support of the government as God-given and God-maintained in the 'good old days' when they had the authority and the captive audiences, that inhibited both Catholic and Protestant Churches in Northern Ireland from raising a prophetic voice, and bringing people back to their senses before it was too late?

In the best sense of the word loyalty involves a self-transcending devotion to the wider group and the larger responsibility, a sense of belonging and commitment, the legitimate pride and strength to be derived from one's own culture and tradition. Where, however, can such loyalty be invested today?

If we take Northern Ireland as a barometer of the British scene as a whole, it is obvious that the very term 'loyalty' drags a long tail of negative connotations: blind obedience, prejudice, emotional solidarity with political parties or personalities, with paramilitary organisations, with one's 'kith and kin'. There are many different scales of loyalty here, based on different myths, different models of authoritarianism. What ultimate or rather penultimate loyalties are to be discerned by the Christian Churches in such a complex situation?

The prophetic witness of the Bible would seem to

44

a *critical solidarity* with the society in which we live. This would exclude the easy options of total identification or of 'privatism'. It would recognise that it has generally been through the small group, the prophetic voice, that the Church has benefited society as a whole in the past, but it would also resist the fasionable and pervasive pessimism about creating a more just society by pointing to the positive forces available to promote renewal: the experience won in countless experiments in community action, for example, or the long British tradition of common-sense democratic interaction. Love of one's neighbour makes a wholly negative attitude to the 'powers that be' impossible. Effective action on behalf of the disadvantaged demands participation in power. In Scotland today, for example, the depth of the current economic and political malaise, especially in the Strathclyde Region, would make any abstention from political involvement seem sheer irresponsibility. Any theology of peace must be relevant to the spiralling threat of violence *in our midst*. We must be involved, but critically so, laying bare the real issues at stake, not shrinking from conflict, but equally determined not to foreclose the possibilities of ultimate reconciliation.

Conclusions

1. The political attitudes of the Church have been characterised throughout its history by quite extraordinary oscillations between deference, defiance and adulation. There is no single 'Christian' attitude.

2. Genuine political indifferentism has not been a mark of the Christian religion. Political autho-

rity was almost always a problem for the Christian Church, the Christian Church a problem for the political authorities.

3. Quietism, the closest Christianity came to indifferentism, in fact often provoked the most violent persecution. In totalitarian situations the Church's insistence on political abstinence gave it room to develop symbolic alternatives to the status quo. In the long run these could prove politically fertile.

4. The assimilationist model, in which Christianity legitimised the political establishment, has been the most prevalent one, usually theologically based on a false understanding of Romans 13. The independent dynamic of Christianity was, however, never totally submerged. On specific issues, e.g. slavery, the prophetic role emerged, and the brutalisation of politics was resisted by reference to divine law.

5. The concordat pattern embraces the worst and the wisest political reflection within the Church. Its realism could be Machiavellian; but it also contributed to the characteristically European mode of resolving conflict: representative government.

6. The rigorist model sometimes underpinned theocracies, but its stress on divine sovereignty could also relativise political authority and foster pluralism.

7. Today the Church appears less inclined either to sacralise or daemonise the political authorities; the focus of interest appears to be moving away from governmental to community level.

8. Appeals to obedience or loyalty are suspect. A

9. There seem to be three possible areas of commitment:

   (a) To those who are our immediate neighbours, whether or not we like them or have chosen them.

   (b) To some future and better society, to a vision of peace and justice which gives us orientation and an incentive to action.

   (c) To the Christian community which already anticipates this hoped-for world in its being and action.

10. Violence and the threat of violence are putting the liberal democratic order under immense strain. This violence, whether manifested in the media, hooliganism, or organised crime, is related to our failure as a nation to resolve fundamental social problems in a way which is, and is seen to be, just.

The Mark of Cain

Is there a fundamental flaw in the universe? Joseph K., in Franz Kafka's *The Trial*, swept into the meshes of a remote, anonymous, faceless machine, never can hope for justice. He cannot even discover what crimes he is supposed to have committed. In Peter Weiss's new dramatic adaptation of the novel, this overwhelming sense of powerlessness is attributed to his bondage to petty-bourgeois norms; others have interpreted it in terms of religious alienation, existential *angst*, or the dehumanisation of modern man by the impersonal social patterns in which he must exist.

Man adrift on a sea of meaninglessness bereft even of the dignity of tragedy. This is the characteristic theme of our contemporary seers.

What has this resurgence of a pessimistic view of man to do with the Christian traditional teaching about original sin? It is very much a Western phenomenon, of course. Is it anything more than fin-de-siècle weariness as Western civilisation lurches away from the centre of the world stage? Is it a fashionable alibi for inaction, non-commitment? It is, after all, the affluent — commanding unprecedented resources — who stress their powerlessness in our contemporary world.

The most curious contradictions appear. Gloomy

prognostications about peace, justice, or even declining moral standards co-exist with a decidedly undented confidence in the private sphere. Within a framework of 'ultimate' pessimism the Western individual proceeds in fact on highly optimistic assumptions about human nature, at least that of his 'nearest and dearest'. Under the nuclear umbrella the march towards self-fulfilment via liberal education and deep inter-personal relations continues. Asceticism of any variety is very much at a discount. The idea of original sin, dubbed indiscriminately 'medieval', or 'Calvinist' is strictly tabu in what one might term progressive circles.

The Churches themselves are rather embarrassed by the doctrine. Talk of the origins of sin and death appears simply to bewilder a generation which, if anything, experience itself as fate-ridden, not guilt-ridden, lost in the impersonal canyons of the cities. Perhaps the refinements of the technology of death we have perfected — in Auschwitz, Dresden, Hiroshima — have shattered the possibility of meaning. For Paul, sin gave death meaning. In death sin found its reward. But for what possible sin can the mass graves of Hamburg or Warsaw be a testimony? Today's ultimate pessimism, unlike the total depravity views of previous generations, is unflanked by any affirmation about an original or natural order which has been violated. Like Original Sin the doctrine of Natural Law carries scant conviction today. Where, if at all, do we discern a degree of natural order in our universe? The liberal utopianism pilloried by Reinhold Niebuhr in *Moral Man and Immoral Society* may have gone for ever, but what have we to substitute for it?

It is interesting that the Churches in the Eastern Europe sphere do not seem to share this pessimism, while the theology emerging from the developing countries, although still highly tentative and contextual in tone, bears many of the marks of a renascence of Christian humanism, of optimism about the future of man, about his dignity and educability.

Within the world Church today, then, we find a wide range of anthropologies, with the West, on the whole, reflecting its own cultural despair, the developing countries their confidence in their future. Optimism, in the West, is reserved for the individual; in the developing countries for society as a whole. The traditional divide of the European theological tradition between the Thomist dialectic of nature and grace and the Lutheran of law and gospel, does not agitate the modern African, Latin American or Asian Christian. He seems often happier with the Old Testament than with Paul and the whole Pauline drama of redemption. If we exclude the late chapters at the very beginning of Genesis, there seems to be very little room in the Old Testament for the concept of original sin. Its winsome, but also brutal naturalness, its embeddedness in social and political issues, help to explain the rediscovery of the historical as well as the prophetic books in much non-Western theology. Take the way, for example, in which Black Theology fastens on the Exodus theme. To what extent is our traditional doctrine of original sin a construct from Platonic metaphysics and Stoic ethics? Is the Christian in the developing countries closer to the Hebraic categories of the Bible? Or is he or she merely blind, at the moment, to the radical depths of evil which we Westerners have dredged in two World Wars?

Before we leap to any too glib conclusions about this, let us re-examine the way in which the doctrine of Original Sin has in fact operated in our Western, European history. We should watch any tendency to see this teaching in isolation from others. It is meaningless to talk of the original sin of Adam, for example, without recognising that the context for such reflection has been whatever is meant by the saving event of the Second Adam. Simplistic pessimism, of the fashionable variety prevalent today, may have very little in common with the authentic Christian tradition.

'It was through one man that sin entered the world, and through sin death, and thus death pervaded the whole human race, inasmuch as all men have sinned.' It is hard to know which is more astonishing: the dominance of Pauline ideas in the early Hellenistic Church, or the speed with which they were consigned to forgetfulness or reverent incomprehension by following generations. From the second century on, Paul's thinking became more and more submerged in a dominant moralism and even rigorism, which owed much to the philosophical schools and the Juoaic synagogue.

It was Augustine's merit to rediscover Paul's views. His formulations, forged in a crisis both personal and political (the Fall of Adam and the Fall of Rome!) have stamped Western theology ever since. The very profundity of his introspection, the depth of his self-understanding, led him to a radical stance on man's corruption which is all too easily misunderstood when applied to more 'ordinary' men. The suggestion too, that original sin is transmitted in the very act of generation has had the most unfortunate influence on the understanding of sex.

Politically, the brilliant apologetic of the *City of God* wrenched Church and theology out of the awesome suction created by the collapsing Roman Empire, by distinguishing firmly between the transient fortunes of secular power and the eternal purposes of the city of God. This was of course necessary enough. It had, however, the unfortunate effect of laying the foundations of Christian political thinking at a time when political power and authority were in the most rapid decline. This does much to explain the Church's rather negative estimate of the function of the state. Political authority, with its coercive sanctions, was regarded as the price of the Fall, of Original Sin, but also as its partial remedy. It kept the worst excesses of human viciousness within certain bounds. As such the Christian had the duty to lend it his support. Roland Bainton, however, quite rightly draws attention to the melancholy nature of this conviction. Engagement in and for 'the world' was laid upon the Christian. But his true goal lay beyond it. Augustine never shook himself free of the neo-Platonic axiom that the material world is to be transcended, if not shunned. The ideal life, in this non-ideal world, is the contemplative one. Political involvement belongs to the moral, not the spiritual realm. The advantage of this attitude is its realism. He has, for example, no time for adulation of the Roman Empire and is aware of the 'grey areas', the unlovely compromises necessary in the life of the statesman.

His famous doctrine of the Just War is a sober attempt to take account of the world as he believed it to be, but without lapsing into resignation. Man, his own worst enemy, can — to some extent — be protected against himself through the over-arching Providence of God. Order can be maintained if war is waged by the due authorities, for a just cause, and within certain limitations. The Sermon on the Mount is spiritualised, interiorised. The important matter is the right motivation. Augustine is all too aware of the death and suffering caused by war, which he does not romanticise. These, however, are not of ultimate importance, like the fate of the soul. We look in vain, therefore, for humanitarian concern. The true Christian is above 'merely human' consideration.

The service rendered by Augustine to the Church as it entered the so-called Dark Ages was considerable. Despite the apparent vacuum of political power the Christian Church, with its virtual monopoly of learning and continuity with the traditions of the past, was preserved from the temptation of despairing altogether of the secular realm. Kings leant heavily on their prince-bishops, and without the civilising work of monasteries Europe would never have arisen at all. The code of chivalry may never have been realised in practice, but our generation is the last to have any right to mock at its achievements in limiting war.

Gradually, however, the melancholy realism of Augustine gave way to a more thorough-going secularisation of the Church. As part of the feudal system, Church structures became rooted in and to the land, the clergy dependent on king and seigneur. To fight off such massive immobilisation new papal, monastic and theological initiatives became necessary, lest the Church be totally submerged by the world around it.

We cannot follow here the long-drawn tussles of Investiture conflicts and reform movements. The point is that it took an *ascetic* movement to rescue Christendom from the stifling embraces of feudalism, an ascetic separation from a sinful world. Nothing could be more misplaced, particularly in our contemporary situation, than the usual Protestant mistake of regarding asceticism and effective action as alternatives.

At its best, as in Thomism, the concern of the medieval Church was to maintain a proper balance between the worlds of nature and supernature. In one Natural Law was conceived to prevail and Aristotelian categories were utilised to make room for a positive assessment of the secular. Aquinas, for example, regarded the political structure as the medium of the popular will. The people were the source of authority and the executive must gain the people's consent. The function of government was not just to contain original sin. With the aid of grace, however, man could transcend the created realm.

There is, then, no question of a dualist rejection of the world, of a rejection, for example, of marriage and civil obligation, such as the Cathari advocated. The 'activist' was necessary as well as the contemplative and had a legitimate pride in his work. On the other hand, the role of ruler or warrior or even peasant (the trader and artisan hardly counted) was as clearly subordinate to that of the spiritual estate as nature to grace, the temporal to the eternal, the pale light of the moon to the life-giving warmth of the sun.

This hierarchy of values assigned the Church a pastoral responsibility for the socio-political realm, a sense of obligation which lies behind the much-criticised Papal theocracy and the Inquisition itself. The tendency is to see the secular area as a potentially anarchic one which has to be contained, by oaths, vows, laws, sanctions, but above all by precept and piety, rather than as one full of possibilities for creative new development. The prominence of juridical features in the medieval church is in large part explained by this need to prevent men endangering their eternal destiny by relapsing into sinful ways. We should, perhaps, resist too quick judgements about paternalism in this context, and pose instead the awkward question of how power can ever be exercised by the Church on others' behalf without endangering the Church itself.

Piety and practice went their different ways in the later medieval period. Piety became increasingly individualistic, manifesting a fixation with sin and death. In the economic growth-points of Italy and the Low Countries, however, and in the emergent nationalism of the Western monarchies, secular motifs became more and more evident. It is hard to resist the conclusion that the relative optimism of the Renaissance about man, for all its undoubted roots in Patristic reflection on the imago Dei, rested on the solid economic and technological achievements which followed urbanisation, the spread of trade, banking and early capitalism. We tend to forget that the Renaissance was almost as productive of new initiatives in the communal as the artistic realm. The idealism of More's *Utopia* was reflected, however, imperfectly, in the civic humanism of Italy, the Tudor emphasis on 'good lordship', the French progress in state-building, but also in the pragmatic, common-sense ethic of the South German cities. Property, family and community were the concerns of the 'men that mattered', the patrician merchants. It was Europe's 'Development era', commercially, geographically, and culturally, that produced some of the finest statements of Christian Humanism ever written. For these were not anti-religious men, only anti-ascetic. Their faith-affirmation took a secular form.

The Reformation (and Counter-Reformation) can be seen as yet another swing of the pendulum, a puritan, or ascetic rejection of humanist values, with a consequent rehabilitation of the doctrine of Original Sin. Luther certainly emphasised the total depravity of man as never before in his teaching on justification by faith alone. Yet he drew his support from the 'secularising' merchant and professional classes. He abandoned the idea of the 'Christian state', arguing instead for the autonomy of the secular realm, and the dignity of the secular vocation. The initial thrust of his 'Two Kingdoms' theory, that of the Gospel and love on the one hand and that of the Law and the sword on the other, was meant to free the socio-political realm from clerical domination. As such it had its liberating aspects.

In practice, however, Luther — like the Counter-Reformation — proved politically and socially reactionary. His aim had been a self-limiting ordinance for the Church. It was to eschew theocracy and simply preach the Gospel to political man. In this way society would be gradually penetrated by the spirit of the Gospel. In fact his predominant concern became that of demarcation. He sought to fence off the secular sphere from 'enthusiasm', e.g. from the attempts of the peasants to draw direct social consequences from the new theology. Such attempts, he believed, denied the essentially gratuitous and spiritual nature of the Gospel, and substituted a new materialism and legalism. It is 'enthusiasm' to forget that in this fallen world the sword, not the precepts of the Gospel, will prevail. Luther's doctrine of original sin thus inhibits any attempt to alter the *structures* of society. As an individual the Christian is bound by the Sermon on the Mount. As prince, judge, soldier, executioner or plain subject his allegiance is to the natural orders of creation, which alone preserve his neighbour and indeed the Christian community as a whole from the ravages of the unprincipled. Thus the doctrine of original sin becomes the basis of a paternalistic and authoritarian understanding of society. Calvinism was rather different. Calvin's particular stress on election rather blunted the edge of the total depravity doctrine as far as the godly community was concerned, and enabled it to develop a more dynamic approach to the structures of society. Indeed, Calvinism's optimism about the role of the law in applying Christian principles to society made it the chosen vessel for the last serious attempts to revive the ascetic principles of medieval Christendom: Puritanism.

Such political creativity as Christianity has had

ceased in the 17th century, about the time when the doctrine of original sin also lost its grip. The new ideas came from outside Church and Theology, from the Enlightenment, the American and French Revolutions, from Marxism. At its best, the Church responded to them. It did not, with the significant exception of the Anabaptist and Quaker 'sects', produce them.

The Anabaptist had agreed with Luther about the sinfulness of 'the world'. His conclusion, however, was that this meant a strict separation from the world for the individual Christian. He must not fight, swear oaths, take disputes to court, or hold civil office. True discipleship was possible only if the Christendom concept was once and for all jettisoned. Again, there is no legitimation here for any onslaught on the structures of society. Quaker optimism about education considerably modified the sharpness of this contrast between godly Christian and sinful world, and encouraged a more than purely symbolic leverage to be exerted on those who exercise power.

Power, or powerlessness, is where we began. The Adam myth, and the story of Babel, like so much else in the Old Testament, betrays a fundamental unease about the exercise of power, much of it quite incomprehensible to 'modern man'. The doctrine of Original Sin can be understood as one long wrestling with this question of power. Do we really want it, or do we fear it? The pursuit and the rejection of power have both been justified in the past. The reasons adduced have seldom been the whole story. We must try to get beyond slogans about 'no compromise', or 'not being afraid to get our hands dirty' to analyse our own motivations for power-seeking or power-shunning. Knowing ourselves, and knowing the thirst for power, we have to learn to structure love. What is the role of the 'powerless' here? How can the small groups from which new initiatives must come be alert to the competitive, power-seeking element within them? How can they break out of their isolation and pave the way for larger, more influential ones? How can we get our social and political structures to flesh out the love of God?

An awareness of the reality of original sin need not encourage passivity, escapism, fatalism. Quite the contrary! By alerting us to the real obstacles to progress, not least those within ourselves, it puts a premium on sane and realistic plans, and hinders a judgemental outlook. In Northern Ireland, for example, para-military groups like the IRA and UDA can be seen as 'caught up in something' far greater than themselves. What they are doing can be regarded with compassion, not anger; the human face of violence can be discerned.

We have, then, to learn how to weave between heaven and earth, rejecting the heresy of perfectionism, but reaffirming the potential for change. In Northern Ireland today the greatest Christian witness is the rejection of pessimism and determinism. To accept these attitudes is basically non-Christian; it is to deny grace. Both fatalism and glib optimism fails to see that 'all creation is groaning with birth pangs'.

The dialectic between realism and hope, between continual destruction (vivid enough in Belfast) and continual resurrection, rests in a theology of the cross. Hope nestles in despair, God in Christ holds all together and starts it all again and again. Original sin, by pointing to the mystery of the cross, indicates the real grounds for hope. In Belfast, for example, among the very few signs of hope are those incidents where people involved in tragic events have reacted with forgiveness. Death as the ultimate shatters our prejudices. Those most involved in bereavement and pain are those with the least bitterness.

The flawed and imperfect world we inhabit is not static. It allows progress to better things. There may sometimes be something of original sin in our very impatience about political action. Teilhard de Chardin argues that we have to assess progress over a very much longer time-scale than that of recorded history, that we are in the midst of a long evolution which points to the future.

In contemporary Britain the evidence of progress is particularly difficult to interpret. On a formal level at least the machinery for change exists still in Britain, in party structures, trade unions and elsewhere. As a system for minimising the abuse of power, and for permitting a degree of power-sharing, British democracy continues to have great merits. Corruption is low, and there is a relatively high degree of transparency in decision-making. An ideal state presupposes ideal people. Democracy, with its checks and balances, is realistic enough to take them as they are. It takes original sin into its calculations!

On the other hand, as Northern Ireland shows, democracy only works where the minority is protected against tyrannisation by the majority. Democracy assumes a moral consensus, a web of traditional values which subtly qualifies the impulsiveness and blinkered vision of the individual voter.

How far does such a consensus still exist? Significant sections of the British people never participate in any sort of power. They never feel that their opinions matter. Frustration and the resort to violence are the inevitable results of this exclusion from real decision-making. Take the social apartheid of a council housing estate like Pilton in Edinburgh. Three boys from Pilton (just one example from the army of those 'born to fail') left school in 1977 with excellent records, but were converted by a humiliating summer of unemployment into truculent vandals and trouble-makers. The signs that our present democratic system is determined or able to remedy such blatant inequalities are hardly encouraging. At best progress towards a more just society seems painfully slow, dependent as it is on the interaction of a bewildering variety of factors, none of them decisive.

A complicating factor is the failure of imagination which restricts people's attention to the immediate orbit of family, locality, and business. Indeed, original sin might be defined as just this inertia of will, mind, emotions, and imagination. Thus we should be cautious about pinning too much faith in direct participatory democracy, valuable as the initiatives in community councils, school councils and health councils may be. One local group might war against the other, with scant regard for the wider community, as is seen every time it is proposed that a hostel for alcoholics, say, or a List D school, be established in a 'desirable' district.

While maximum *participation* in decisions by the maximum number of people is desirable, it is far from obvious that the mere counting of heads is the best way of settling questions, especially when they require specialist knowledge or, like capital punishment, arouse strong emotions. Increasingly the complexities of trade agreements or energy policies are above the heads of most people. At what point does democratic competence stop and that of the expert take over? The question of the future use of nuclear energy is likely to pose this dilemma in the sharpest way.

None of our current models of democracy, then, seems to have the monopoly of wisdom, if the aim is to remedy the structural injustices in society, one of the manifestations of original sin. The democrat tends to think of justice as a balance, as an equal and rational distribution of scarce resources. The Biblical understanding of justice, the action of God on behalf of the oppressed, sets rather different accents.

Liberation theology, which embodies this Biblical insight, may well be more applicable to Britain than is usually thought, and our allergic reaction to any mention of revolutionary remedies for our society should be coolly analysed.

This emergency of liberation theology, and of its European counterpart, political theology, may yet prove to be the most creative Christian political initiative since Puritanism in the seventeenth century. Its integration into the patterns of life and thought of the British Churches poses an enormous challenge and offers the most exciting of possibilities for their renewal.

Although often accused of not having read the Bible or thought out their theology, and of taking no account of sin, in fact the liberation writers distinguish clearly between political liberation and the Kingdom of God. The first is only the anticipation of the other. The exact relationship can be formulated in different ways. Official Catholic theology, for example, would be unhappy with the term 'anticipation'. Others would see the Kingdom of God as an extension of the society produced by Christian liberation. For all, however, the distinction is clear.

Nor is the liberation theologian a utopian idealist. He does not claim to have a full vision of the just society. He begins, rather, with the perversion of all political action and structures by sin, and in this confused situation — and confusion is part of sin — he perceives something specific and then acts on it, as Martin Luther King did, for example. The social dimensions of sin are recognised. To break through the vicious spiral of failure and discrimination, to terminate the continual falling short of the mark, 'missing the point', the liberation theologian looks to the righteousness so often stressed by the Old Testament. In one of the most fascinating reversals in theological history the Old Testament is brought in to redress the New (or, rather, an individualistic misunderstanding of the New). The sin of Adam who, as Romans 5 says, has 'missed the point', is met not with fatalism but with a call to justice or righteousness (the one Greek word must do service for both).

Thus the doctrine of original sin, the sin of Adam, which for such long tracts of the Church's history effectively under-pinned paternalist and authoritarian politics, now re-emerges in Liberation Theology as the analytical tool which highlights the tension between the human condition as it is and the vision of ultimate justice.

Conclusions.

1. Genuine concern for the disadvantaged and impoverished, whether at home or abroad, has to come to terms with the powerful forces within our society, partly financial, partly industrial, and partly militarist, which very successfully resist the radical redeployment of resources.

2. The just peace we strive for will always be defective, for there is something in us which distorts our best plans.

3. We have, therefore, to walk a razor's edge between patience, not least with ourselves, and impatience at the intolerable injustice around us.

4. The pressing problem is not how to devise abstract models of a just society but how to effect the transition from less to more human relationships within our given situation.

5. The small, close-knit Christian group has special responsibilities and opportunities for forging initiatives and spreading awareness of non-violent avenues to justice and peace.

A Forward Looking Faith

'Who will change the world? Those who dislike it.' Bertold Brecht

'Cease to dwell on days gone by and to brood over past history.
Here and now I will do a new thing.' Isaiah 43.18

Today books with titles like *Religion, Revolution and The Future* roll off the press every month. The rediscovery of the forward-looking dimension of Christianity within the past decade has done more, however, than turn theology upside down. Because of its actual rootage in the life experience of the suffering Church it is threatening to turn the piety and practice of the Church upside down as well. Since the Reformation nothing like this has happened. More and more theory and practice are allying to prise the Church out of its ease in a diseased world, and quite new confessional questions are being posed, with sovereign disregard for the old denominational frontiers. Unprecedented conflicts can be expected in the next few years as both sides begin to realise the full implications. The sullen, but also more subtle resistance of establishment Christianity is already gathering way.

The new theologies of hope, of liberation, of development signify that the day of the *Kulturkampf*, whether in its Roman Catholic or Barthian form, is over. The massive 'No' of the Syllabus of Errors and of Barmen to the nationalistic perversion of Christianity has been replaced or complemented by an equally massive 'Yes' to solidarity with the international struggle for justice. All manner of consequences follow. The crisis of theology, discerned since the 1930s in the personal encounter of the individual, is increasingly being related to the realm of peace and justice. Biblical exegesis is being nudged out of its professional ghettos. Above all, politics is being lifted out of the grip of unproductive moralising and placed firmly in the context of the Gospel we have to offer the world, into the forefront of theological concern.

Nothing could be more surprising. Albert Schweitzer's conclusions about the altogether alien character of early Christian apocalyptic was mirrored by the man in the pew's embarrassment at the weird language and disappointed expectations associated with the Second Coming. Preaching about it was left to the 'nuts' and the sects. As the pendulum swings in the opposite direction today we should keep this old bewilderment firmly in mind, lest we land with a new glib orthodoxy.

It is, after all, most remarkable that what appears to be the most mythological and unworldly aspect of the Biblical message — its preaching of the imminent end of the world — should be powering the chariot of revolutionary politics. As we shift our focus from original sin to 'eschatology', from origins to ultimates, beginnings to ends, it is the theodicy question, the dilemma of evil in a God-created world, which provides the red thread of continuity. If Genesis saw pain, toil and death as the just punishment for sin, Revelation envisages the coming of Christ in power as the vindication of the oppressed. Apocalyptic is thus the last Biblical fruit of the sustained refusal of Israel, old or new, to drop the shutters on passionate concern about the 'home of identity' (Bloch), about peace, justice and the cruel reality of their present absence.

We learn through life, not books. Israel's prophetic Messianism was the bastard child of a hated and hateful exile. Those who wept by the waters of Babylon could no longer celebrate in the great festivals the fulfilled promise of land and security to a once-enslaved people. The backward-looking covenant theme of happier days was gone for ever. Stripped of privilege and far from Zion, eyes turned again to the future, to a New Covenant, to a sobered remnant who might again hope for peace and justice.

Within the world Church today the critique of tradition and the revival of eschatological pers-pectives has also been born in the womb of exile. The Churches of the West and of Eastern Europe, a sobered remnant, have had to adjust themselves to the reality of a post-Christendom, post-Constantinian era. Daily their real stake in the past diminishes, though the prevalence of nostalgia may still disguise this in suburban Britain. Simultaneously the Churches in the developing countries are realising how minimal their stake is in the present state of affairs. Almost miraculously there is a growing consensus on the ecumenical level between Christians from rich and poor nations at a time when they might well be expected to be drifting apart.

The fragility of this consensus, however, scarcely needs underlining. In our dream-washed land few recognise themselves yet for the remnant that they are, and nowhere is the chasm between ecumenical thinking and the ordinary church member so evident as on just this question of eschatological perspectives. Global interdependence may simply mean an awesome escalation of conflict between privileged and under-privileged. The Church will have to know where it stands in this situation. Is it enmeshed in the myths and privileges of the past? Is its stance towards the future one of apprehension, or one of hope? Has its very wealth of insight and history and tradition become its most crippling burden?

Our difficulties with eschatology are legion. It is virtually impossible for us to appreciate or understand the original impact of the coming and going of Jesus on men's understanding of time. Obviously it shattered their cosmos, telescoping or foreshortening the anticipated stretch of the generations into the compass of one or two decades, catapulting the ultimate future into the immediacy of present expectation. The 'at handness' of the Kingdom liberated from all other concerns for security, success, even survival itself. New forms of service, community and reflection burgeoned. The early Christian slept with his or her eschatological boots on.

The disappointment at the non-arrival of the parousia, of the Second Coming, can hardly be conceived. It has stamped orthodox Christianity ever since with disillusion about the future. It was never again to risk such a let-down. Resignation took the form of closing the Canon, tightening up on discipline, absolutising the Apostolic past. Betrayed by the future, it found solace in elaborating its myths of origin.

The rasping dialectic between Old Israel and New

Israel, Old Covenant and New Covenant, heroically maintained by Paul, proved impossible to sustain. By dint of judaising the New Testament and allegorising the Old Testament, the eschatological tension was rendered harmless, and the Church settled down in the world. It mocked the Jews, still looking to the future for their Messiah, and so evidently in exile from their beloved Jerusalem, their dispersion and lowly status a sure sign of the divine wrath.

For its part Christianity followed the lead of Augustine in substituting a high doctrine of the Church for the expectation of the millennium. Why reach forward with yearning to the future when in the Church itself the Kingdom has already found virtual realisation? Historically, 500-1500 A.D. was in fact to be the millennium of the *Church*. The old millennial expectation never died out completely, but on the whole it was the heretics who represented it.

The consequences were grave. Eschatological expectation became associated with unorthodoxy and schism, with rebellion against the authority of the Church as well as the values of society. This fostered inertia within the institutional Church. It also left the apocalyptic tradition in the hands of sociologically and intellectually narrow and often desperate groupings. We cannot, of course, blame this development on theology alone. Anchored to the land by feudalism the churches became the hill-shrines of a society which venerated security above all else, perhaps because in reality there was so little security to be had. Even monasticism, that great bodying-out of the eschatological dream of perfect community, came to personify *stabilitas* in its dominant Benedictine form.

It was the casualties of society who kept the millennial dream alive, the victims of plague, famine, war and of the unacceptable face of early urbanisation. From the 11th century over-population began to create a floating population of the discontented. Wandering prophets found ready listeners among them when they interpreted the woes of the present as the birth-pangs of a better and juster age. The apocalyptic visions of *Daniel* and *Revelation*, the dark predictions of the so-called Sibylline Oracles with their political overtones, above all Joachim of Fiore's preaching of an imminent Age of the Spirit, expressed the despair and anger of the impoverished. The call to the crusades, directed at the address of the chivalric cream of society, stirred unlooked-for responses and plumbed unsuspected depths. Ragged journeymen, bands of shepherds and herdsmen, even children set off on hopeless, horrible pilgrimages to wrest Jerusalem from Anti-Christ. En route they purged the land of worldly clerics and incinerated the Christ-murdering Jew — obstacles all to the coming of the millennium. Many were slaughtered by the alarmed authorities; most perished miserably. The thousand year *Reich* of innocence and justice had to exact its toll of blood.

There is a veritable obsession with blood in these millennial groupings. After the Black Death in the 14th century, the flagellants provided their strange variation on the theme. Only blood could cleanse. The Christian communism of the Taborites of Bohemia revived the bloody traditions of the Old Testament holy war and ban. The Brethren of the

Free Spirit combined a cult of Adamic innocence with brutal amoralism. In Renaissance Florence troupes of 'angelic' youths rampaged through the city in support of Savonarola's crusade against Babylonic Rome. In the 1520s Thomas Müntzer urged his covenanted army of peasants and artisans to apocalyptic violence, and the same godly ruthlessness made the city of Münster a byword a few years later.

Such millenarian excesses cannot simply be dismissed as the fantasies of a bygone age. The cult of an absolutised innocence did not cease with the French Revolution: "Par pitié, par amour pour l'humanité, soyez inhumains!" The nuclear armouries of today are manned by immaculately dressed, clean limbed 'boys'. Armageddon, when it comes, will be monstrously hygienic.

Nor can we be blind to the danger of raising expectations that cannot be fulfilled. In the case of Savonarola and the Reformers the preaching of Old Testament prophecy and New Testament Gospel proved social dynamite. The folly and agony of the great Peasants War is increased, not diminished, by its utopian and Christian dimensions. Prince and patrician ensured that its cry for divine justice must be abortive. A just peace was never on the horizon. Indeed the mobilisation of peasant forces offered the forces of reaction the most welcome of pretexts for crushing rural dissidence once and for all.

The Reformation continued the orthodox medieval tradition of consigning eschatology to the periphery of theological concern. The eschatological motif so prominent in early Lutheranism was comfortably spiritualised; justification by faith was preached to captive audiences from a paternalistic pulpit. Similarly the Council of Trent and the Counter-Reformation assumed the God-given nature of the existing structures of society. Never again was Europe to be so Christian as after the religious revival of Reformation and Counter-Reformation. The last Jew had been bundled out of Spain. Protestant and Catholic censors vied with one another in severity. Erasmians were on the run, the witch-craze reached a new level of intensity, gentle Anabaptists gurgled their way to a drowning death. Fortunately, the poisonous hostility between Catholic and Protestant prevented the total disappearance of pluralism. Neither side quite succeeded in imposing a hermetic seal on their godly societies, but the violence they used to maintain 'the peace' is quite as impressive as the violence of the millenarians in pursuing justice.

Certainly the 17th century proved neither just nor peaceful. Its religious wars scunnered Europe with confessional Christianity once and for all. Yet millennial revivals produced philo-Semitism and contributed to the social radicalism of the revolution in England. Geographically, scientifically, philosophically, Europe was bursting its bonds and bounds. We still know remarkably little about the dynamics of modernisation. What we do know is that our secular, pluralist, technologically and industrially inventive society has its roots in the 17th century. No non-Christian civilisation has ever produced anything like it, and while triumphalist Christian apologetics may be treated with due caution, objectivity demands that we examine why this should be so.

Christianity has had a remarkable tradition of

hospitality to rational enquiry. The conventional wisdom of today notes the intolerance of Calvinist or Jesuit, but is strangely blind to their passionate rationality, and their zeal for education. The disciplined readiness for the wilderness, the restless quest for paradise are, for example, eschatological motifs whose importance for Puritan scholarship G. H. Williams has demonstrated. Again and again, often against the whole weight of the institutional Church, the Christian faith has engendered acids of criticism which dissolved in time the sociological or ideological casings within which it once appeared so irrevocably confined — even the casing of 'Christian civilisation' itself. As Georges Khodre puts it, there is within the Church a 'catastrophic dimension' which challenges every settled order and demands 'a constant acceleration of achievement.'

The relevance of this liberating critique, this cerebral Pentecostalism, to our theme of peace and justice should be clear enough. For as we enter the revolutionary era in European history at the end of the eighteenth century it is not enough to recognise the generally negative stance of Christian theology and churchmanship: the holy trinity of tradition, religion and authoritarianism. We must also recognise the other side.

Hannah Arendt, in her essay on *Revolution*, insists on the radical novelty of the experience of being free which the French and American revolutions produced. Based on a belief in man's natural goodness (Rousseau) or on self-evident truths about the rights of man (Jefferson), this represented a total departure from Christianity's doctrine of original sin, its cyclical view of history, its supernaturalist transcendentalism. She highlights, too, the way in which the revolutions betrayed their ideals. In the French Revolution compassion gives way to rage, the proclamation of freedom to a grim doctrine of historical necessity. Likewise the American experiment degenerates into a bourgeois protection of private rights, and in Russia the Marxist dream of freedom fades into the promise of affluence.

These manifest flaws in the revolutionary programmes need not blind us to their grandeur. This very grandeur, however, is strangely interwoven with the Christian tradition, which had never lost sight of the dream of natural innocence. The Classical Golden age, in itself only a nostalgic evocation of a possibility for ever forfeit, gained acute relevance when yoked to Christian eschatology. Was the kingdom of peace and justice perhaps, after all, the natural destiny of man? Was the universal salvation, *apocatastasis*, the ultimate end of the experiment of human history? Repeatedly — before, after, and during the Revolutions — such hopes continued to surface.

None of this reflects much credit on the Christian Church since the dreamers generally had to emigrate outside it to gain a hearing. The extraordinary aspect of our present situation is that it seems to represent a belated appropriation of the themes of Christian eschatology *within the Christian community itself*. The subversive potential of the central doctrines of creation and redemption to any and every moral and political order is being realised, from *creatio ex nihilo* to *justificatio impiorum* to *resurrectio mortuorum*. The dead are to be raised, the godless vindicated, nothingness is to become

76

life-engendering! What a nightmare this to the social technocrat, the consensus politician, to the myth-maker of the consumer society! Liberation is promised from the incomplete visions of the past, the impersonal restraints of bureaucracy and technology, the seductive lie of powerlessness. The future is open. We are not imprisoned in a web of necessity. God is the freedom of our future.

The polemical edge of the eschatological critique of society is clearer than its positive content. What does it mean to talk of the coming of Christ in the context of world development, or of Ulster, or of the endemic violence in society? We are clearly not making predictions about a thousand year kingdom of the saints to begin on a certain date at a certain place. But what are we saying? Are we simply spiritualising 'Christ' to mean our aspirations in terms of peace and justice? The woolly and inflated rhetoric often found at this point masks some pretty fundamental uncertainties.

Perhaps it is the presence of Anti-Christ and the challenge to contend with him that best signposts the future coming. Cross the divide between the developed world and the poor nations, or between private housing and council schemes, and one sees the medieval frescoes of the Last Judgement in contemporary form. Drive through the shattered streets of confessionally divided Belfast. To say 'Christ is come' becomes a pietistic perversion. One can, however, remembering the glorified myths of the past and the fears of an unknown future, believe and act on the belief that Christ is coming, the same Christ who at present walks incognito in the ranks of the naked and the mourning.

In Belfast the main danger is escapism, a constant tendency to withdraw from the harsh world and look upwards to God. Such escapism can literally keep one alive at times. 'How do you forget?' is the question on everyone's lips. Catholics and Protestants have found their different ways of forgetting. In rural Catholic Ireland you escape through humour, the humour at the wakes, for example. Protestants escape by dogged observance of the law. Both Presbyterian morality and Catholic ritual reflect times past — when Presbyterians were second class citizens and Catholics third class. In that oppressed situation both had made a real contribution.

But how can such past tradition work itself out in the *future*? How can one avoid nostalgic myths, on the one hand, without squandering the priceless heritage of Irish culture, language and history, on the other? For there is a profound sense in which we are 'held' in our traditions, and to abandon them is to abandon our very selves. Somehow we have to wrestle nostalgic myths into the shape of future possibilities.

In Belfast the myth of freedom makes people do desperate things. We have to help people to set the long struggle for freedom in Ireland in its global perspective, to relate it to the Biblical concept of justice and peace, without abandoning the dream of a better, fairer society. The resignation of the pietist is as un-Biblical as the violent activism of the paramilitary groups.

We are not encouraged, by either the Old Testament or the New, to expect this course to be an easy one. Isaiah 53 talks of a suffering servant, not of a King of Glory, and makes as hard reading for us today as for Israel long ago. Jesus did not raise expectations about a perfect society to come in this world. Our vision is fragmentary. We must follow such light as is given in the *actual situation* in which we find ourselves. Is not Christianity always about the present, albeit a present carried by some sense of the future, so that the past is always under judgement, history constantly being re-written, myth re-actualised in novelty, tradition re-realised in creativity? The passage from the Mass is relevant here: 'Christ has died, Christ has risen, Christ will come again'. Past, present, and future all have to be held in balance.

How do we relate such openness to the future to the present reality of the institutional Church? In Ireland, as in Britain as a whole, its strength is often equated with its privileged status in society. It is an obstacle to the transition to a more just society. Its alliance with the state means that men like Terry O'Keefe and Father Desmond Wilson, who challenged its present role, are simply ignored or forced out. The bland statements of the leaders of the four main Churches in Ulster whenever a crisis occurs contribute little to the resolution of the real conflicts.

Jeremiah thought there would never be a forward movement until the Temple was destroyed. Are we trying to preserve something God wants to go? Should this be a time of smashing? Are we really only shoring up a bad situation, with caring organisations like the Vincent de Paul Society for example, so that the structures are not upset? Are we willing to accept the status of a powerless, oppressed group? In the early Church light broke through not to individuals, but to listening, sharing groups. Is our most urgent task to gather a new *body* of people, committed not to the survival of the Churches but to the survival of hope?

Conclusions.
1. The eschatological perspective commits the Christian to revolutionary change.
2. The only question is about the appropriate mode to effect that change.
3. It is easy to storm the future in the name of justice, but only a gentle wooing can coax from the future the reality of justice.
4. The Gospel cannot be identified with any political ideology or system, of the West or the East, of the North or the South.
5. The freedom of the Church, as it operates within the limitations of such ideologies and systems, is its bondage to a greater future.

A Groundswell of Change

'Behold also the order that God hath put generally in all his creatures beginning at the most
inferior or base and ascending upward ... so that
every kind of tree, herbs, birds, beasts, and fishes
are disposed so that in everything is order and
without order may be nothing stable or permanent.' Sir Thomas Elyot.

There is a groundswell of great change in the world
and in the Churches. These changes imply, and
require us to articulate a corresponding change of
perspective. The sort of perspective involved is
indicated within the Roman Catholic tradition by
the call of Vatican II not to be content 'with a
merely individualistic morality', and by the Pope's
recent guarded acceptance of a theology of liberation (*Evangelii Nuntiandi*, esp. pars 14, 30-31).
Within Protestantism the influence of liberation
theology is also strong, especially outside Britain.
There is a shift away from the established Church
towards some contemporary equivalent of a 'Confessing Church'.

This change is by no means discernible every-
where. The Church as a whole lags behind the
advances in theological understanding, and in the
institutional sense has yet to be affected. In Britain,
apart from a few scattered individuals and groups,
the groundswell of change seems to have bypassed
the Churches. A strong conservative reaction is
sometimes more apparent. Yet people no longer
simply accept their place in the Church; they ask
what purpose it serves and what is required of them
as members. This groundswell of change may be
greatest in the Catholic Church.

One vital element in the change of perspective is a new sense of the relationship of sacred and secular. More and more the sacred is seen as the inwardness, the 'within' of the secular, the deepest meaning of the secular. World and Church are not seen as two opposing blocs or powers but as two aspects of the one thing. On such a view the world has no destiny other than that of the Church, and vice-versa, the Church can be said to be the world groping for its own identity.

This understanding of the Church as the 'sacrament' of the world, with the calling to gather in all that is true, authentic and good in the world, is in no way a denial that many outside the Church are involved in this groping, responsive to Jesus, but not to the Church as such, but it is a statement from within the Church as to what it ought to be.

This positive evaluation of earthy, secular reality has arisen particularly from within Western Christianity — part of its inheritance from Judaism — and differentiates it from the other great religions of the world, in which the sacred has a quite different role.

Within this change of perspective we have to try to relate our own domestic, parish-pump concerns to the great world forces. Technology has invaded our kitchens, bureaucracy our offices. How do we track the inter-connections, relate our eating-habits to world hunger, our industrial developments to the under-development of others? We have to learn to see, and in detail, how the development of each man involves the development of all men. In the United States the slavery abolitionists argued that if some were unfree all were unfree and conversely that the liberation attained by one is shared by all. You cannot maintain solidarity in suffering and deny solidarity in liberation.

When we begin to track such inter-connections it soon emerges that a multiplicity of factors are involved. There is no single, easy answer to the injustice in the world; the 'disease' we are probing may turn out to be complex, polymorphous. The Church has both a pastoral and a prophetic role. On the one hand, it has to reassure the alarmed and prepare people for change, on the other hand, to alert them to see how world events grow out of the aggregate of everyone's actions and attitudes, and point to certain overriding issues crying to heaven for correction, such as world hunger, racial discrimination, the arms race. It will not be easy. Very few as yet recognise the urgency of change. For example, an excellent report prepared for the Church of Scotland on the peaceful use of nuclear energy has found disappointingly little resonance.

What, then, is the peculiar contribution of the Churches and of the individual Christian to the attainment of a more just, and more humane world? Is our way that of the 'long trek through the institutions', pursuing positions of power and influence where we can contend against the forces of inertia and exercise some leverage for change? Does our commitment to secularity imply a respect for the secular values of success, effectiveness, productivity? Or is our way that of kenosis or self-emptying, cross-like failure, powerlessness? Northern Ireland, in particular, forces us to address ourselves to the meaning of failure, to engage in a painful stock-taking of our religious and political inheritance.

God, in the Bible, speaks supremely to those who recognise how pathetic they are. Good men and good movements which fail are two a penny in Northern Ireland. What have we to learn from this?

Is the specific Christian attitude to planting a better world one of a *doing* which proceeds from a *being* which is self-emptied, without personal ambition? Have we to bend all our energies to building the house of the world but to do so from within an interior attitude of progressive poverty of spirit and detachment? It seems a tall order!

For all this we need vision. We need a lead. We need to know where we are going.

In the rest of the Christian world, on the Continent, in Africa and Asia, in the Americas, this need has been most notably filled by a revamping of the whole Christian vision around the 'organising concept' of liberation. In the liberation theologies of South America and the political theology of Continental theologians like Moltmann and Metz the vicious circles of economic, political and cultural deprivation from which people suffer are interpreted as the social forms of sin. Gospel and Church are seen as redeeming men not only from private sinfulness but from the all-embracing experience of alienation in an inhuman world, so that they can combat their crippling sense of meaninglessness and godforsakenness.

Liberation Theology

Liberation Theology offers symbols of hope to a humanity enmeshed in the snares of social sin. This is what the Old Testament and the New Testament is all about. If the Gospel is good news for man and the whole of creation then man's struggle for justice, for peace, cannot be in vain. Socialism, democracy and emancipation are symbols for the liberation theologian of man's destined freedom — economic, political and cultural. The kingdom of God is not 'another world', but this world renewed and transformed in the light of the Gospel message and its good news for the poor.

Thus the relief of oppression, as the Old Testament makes so clear, is more than a secular, political concern. It is the demand of faith itself. Faith has to relate to the whole drama of history and not just to the private religious realm. It has to relate to the immediate situation of the believer and not just to pious generalities. It has to be committed, ready to take sides with the down-trodden, though in a spirit of tolerance and reconciliation. What gives liberation theology its cutting edge is this realistic concern with the obedience of faith.

Is this concept of liberation the most useful, binding, inspiring one for our struggles in the British situation, too? Because it derives from the South American situation, it has been seen as 'provincial', with limited applicability to Britain. It has been regarded as 'reductionist' equating the Gospel with politics and the Church with a glorified pressure group. Its lack of spirituality has been regretted. It has also been suggested that, at the least, it requires to be complemented by an equal stress on reconciliation.

All these comments and criticisms have to be taken seriously, although we should be on the watch for the way in which allegedly theological objections can sometimes disguise a more human reluctance to move away from well-trodden paths. The chief danger is probably a too glib acceptance of the 'jargon' of the liberation theologians. In Ulster, for example, terms like liberation and reconciliation have little meaning. All such abstract conceptuality has to be tested against the actual realities.

In our concluding chapters, therefore, the attempt will be made to earth the ideas of liberation theology in the British situation, in Ulster where the dream of liberation has become the wilderness, in the Third World and especially Southern Africa, and in the faith-language and life-style of all of us.

The great ground-swell of change which sweeps us all along is not just something to be endured, ridden out in stoic fortitude as 'future shock'. The theological challenge is to relate it to the eschatological dreams of the prophets of the Old Testament and the apostles of the New, so that we can find ourselves pointed beyond anything we now know or can possibly even imagine. In our search and struggle for the peace of a just society, for 'shalom', we may have to be prepared to leave our received culture, norms and nations and enter a phase of homelessness before we arrive in the land of Canaan.

Conclusions.
1. Politically, the Christian Gospel means liberation.
2. Liberation begins with self; only the free can liberate.
3. Liberation which ends with self is mere pietism or mysticism.
4. As yet the credibility of the Church in Britain as a liberating force is not high.

Violence in Northern Ireland

'To melt suffering into a grain of knowledge for oneself and a joy for others is to shake off false ambitions and abandon all fear.' Janusz Korczak

Nowhere is the question of violence more sharply focussed in the UK than in Northern Ireland. The political humiliation and horrendous human consequences of our failure there have made it very natural that our first reaction — those of us in Scotland, England or Wales — is to turn the blind eye, shrug the shoulder in incomprehension, and treat the TV documentaries as a variation on the spaghetti Western. The ignorance and apathy about Northern Ireland in Britain as a whole is quite incredible.

This bemused indifference, however, is paralleled by the most 'decisive action' of a political and military nature. Stormont has been suspended, constitutional government replaced by direct rule, the British army units in Northern Ireland have been massively reinforced. For many on the mainland this armed intervention salves our consciences. We are 'doing our bit' to hold the divided communities apart and prepare the way for the re-establishment of peace.

The question is: What sort of peace? What is meant by the 'just peace' in Northern Ireland? Would we have preferred the pre-1968 situation to have continued? Would the 'peace' of the period prior to 'the Troubles' have been preferable to the present position? It is a bleak and thorny question.

We would be considerably less than human if we did not wish that 'the Troubles' had never arisen. Yet, for all the human agony and waste and wreckage they brought with them the situation now is potentially far more hopeful. This is not in any way to excuse or forget the outrages still etched on our minds. Quite the contrary. But it is to say that for the first time a just peace may be on the horizon in Northern Ireland, and that, as the standard-bearer of hope, the Church has a peculiar responsibility to point this out.

Paradoxically, the very destruction in Ulster has in some ways cleared the way for new creative beginnings. Since 'the Troubles' there have been more possibilities than ever before for genuine discussion between Catholics and Protestants on matters of faith. The old confessional divide has been partly replaced and partly relativised by the burgeoning of new parties and divisions.

In the political realm, the old Unionist synthesis of Church and State has gone for ever, as men like William Craig have come to realise. New working-class spokesmen have emerged. The old-style politicians have lost both their power as 'fixers' and their credibility. The future may lie with cooperatives, and with grass-root movements which bypass the politicians. It is worth remembering that even power-sharing was imposed from above. Certainly the old political establishments have crashed to the ground and will never be resurrected.

Peace is within our grasp in Northern Ireland, but not the unjust peace which pertained prior to 1968. Professions of concern about violence in Northern

Ireland are totally worthless if they seek to shuffle by that fact. It is the full Christian concept of shalom, of the righteous peace, which is relevant here, not just the cessation of overt hostilities. Such a peace, born out of all the broken hearts and bodies of Ulster, would indeed be a gift to the whole of humanity.

Let us return, though, to the present realities. All the main Churches condemn violence. Yet the para-military groupings continue to attract considerable popular, grass-roots support. Why does the spectacle of Catholic and Protestant leaders jointly denouncing violence fail to carry more conviction?

The reasons, of course, are complex, and it hardly needs re-iteration here that such calls do attract very wide support. One obvious factor limiting Church influence is the growing alienation of the urban working-class from the Churches. It has been estimated that less than fifty per cent of the children in Belfast are now being baptised. The Catholic and Protestant para-military groups are, to a large extent, no longer Church-goers, and listen only to what they want to hear from the Churches. Another increasingly clear point is the futility of platform proclamations. The generalised rhetoric of the Churches about peace lacks credibility as long as they continue to block new initiatives on concrete issues like mixed marriages, for example. Each partner in a mixed marriage is expected to remain in his or her own confessional 'box'. There is a constant attempt to yank one back into one's *own* community. While this 'blackbird mentality' prevails, it is hard to see how the Churches have any right to preach flexibility and generosity to others.

Again, the Churches' condemnation of violence appears very selective. The ordinary man in the Shankill or in Ballymurphy notes that the violence of the British army is not criticised, that there is no critique of the 'just war', that on Remembrance Sunday the Churches are full. The line between 'legitimate' and 'illegitimate' violence drawn by the Churches is interpreted as one more indication of their alignment with the conservative forces in society. Is it violence as such to which the Churches are opposed, or only 'un-constitutional' violence? No clear moral imperative seems to emerge.

From within the Churches, however, there is beginning to emerge — as yet in a tentative way and restricted to individuals and small groups — an awareness that a new approach is necessary. Instead of moralising from an institutional dug-out, a servant Church can stand in repentant solidarity with its people, a Biblical Church can offer its own distinctive analysis of the nature of violence, a forward-looking Church can anticipate the new humanity by putting itself constantly at risk. This chapter's reflections on violence illustrate this concern of Northern Ireland Christians to develop a deeper understanding of the roots and nature of violence by drawing on Biblical and historical perspectives.

The prevalence of violence in human history points to a destructive force in man, a lust for power and possession which leads straight to nihilism. We have to rethink Genesis IV in these terms. Cain's act of violence leads to his enslavement; in destroying we are destroyed.

The wresting of power or possessions from someone else becomes invested with ultimate importance.

Once we have gained this limited objective or that, once we have snatched power we have 'won'. Nationalist movements can be seen as one example of this. Irish nationalism fought to gain power, but not for the Republic of Ireland as it now exists. Similarly the obsession of the capitalist with 'getting to the top', or the seizure of power by Communist movements. It is relatively easy to engineer the coup or the palace revolution, but desperately difficult to prevent the pursuit of power becoming an end in itself. The point soon comes when success turns sour, when we despise what we have come to possess. The next step is nihilism, for there is nothing left to possess.

There is the closest relation between such nihilism and the revolutionary crusade. Why not destroy what is regarded as valueless? Where life is seen as the vomit of a hated, alien environment it is pointless to cherish it, or to attempt to improve it. The petty vandal and the ruthless revolutionary are two sides of the same coin. People are swept aside. Suffering and death are of secondary, soon of no importance. 'The cause' devours everything in its path.

Violence has many different aspects. There is *crude, physical violence*. There is *unthinking violence* — the act of an undisciplined person. *Organised violence* is directed towards a specific end. *Economic violence* is seen in the business world, and in the exploitation of the developing countries. *Built-in-violence* is excused by the need for law and order, e.g. the use of torture in Northern Ireland after internment. *Propaganda violence* is another form, the psychological pressure to conform. In the West this battle for the mind is more hidden, violence being done to our intelligence and integrity. The *'violence' of non-violence* employs intolerable pressure to force others to yield. Violence needs a victim. It is dependent on the passivity of the exploited. Those who actually have to 'execute' violence are usually themselves sufferers from it. The young paratroopers on the streets of Belfast only walk high when their officers are absent. When the officers are there, they simply do not exist. To realise this is to lose all fear of them, and violence only erupts where there is fear.

The alternative to violence

Since violence is almost universally present it is no answer to replace one regime with another. There is always the danger that when you throw out the one devil you let in ten more. You create a political or religious vacuum in which violence thrives because people have no transcendent loyalties, no objectives beyond themselves.

The real challenge to the revolutionary is to present an objective that cannot be possessed, that cannot become an idol. 'It was ourselves that brought us out of Egypt, therefore let us build a golden calf...' The alternative to violence lies in the choice of the truly adequate objective, an objective that cannot be achieved or possessed by us.

This ultimate objective can be defined as the Kingdom of God. Here violence is of no account. Attempts to storm it by violence, such as the Spanish Inquisition, or Protestant persecution of Catholics are always abortive. If we commit ourselves to the Kingdom of God we are already in possession of something that is indestructible, and the ineffectiveness of violence is apparent.

This is not to advocate an otherworldly quietism, but to define the perspective from which the Christian must try to scrutinise all his social and political engagement.

This Kingdom, which we can possess and yet not possess, appears to mean the repudiation of destruction and the encouragement of creativity. In a disposable society we need to urge people not only to conserve but to create, to be co-workers with God, as in Genesis.

The difficulty is the translation of all this into practice, into the realities of community life. Jesus brought the positive right into the actual situation at ground level. What we must do is get people to see that there is an alternative to violence. We have to realise the hope of the situation where we are. God's point of view is that evil is always transformable to a greater good.

Yet while we condemn violence is there a time when destruction becomes inevitable? Unjust power structures have to be removed. How can that be done, how can vested interests be dislodged, clamant injustice cleared away, without at least material destruction, or the threat of violence? How can we learn to go and do what needs to be done and not trample on others in the meantime? How can we avoid capitulating to violence on the one hand, or to the status quo on the other? One thing is certain. The Churches themselves must adopt a more penitent stance. So often in the past they have themselves become implicated in the injustice by standing by and doing nothing. Take the countless examples of teenagers or mere children turning to vandalism and robbery because they had nowhere to go, and nothing to do. We are 'the violent ones' in failing to provide alternatives for the young people. We condemn teenage drinking but where else is there to go than the pubs? Yet youth clubs, theatre groups frequently perish because the Church, one of the institutions which could provide alternatives, is too concerned about its respectable image.

Is the institutional Church in Northern Ireland beyond all hope of the radical reformation necessary for such a change in attitudes? Freedom of speech, and thought, and action are still systematically curtailed. A just peace in Northern Ireland would mean the right of free speech and thought, and the abandonment by the Churches of all their privileges. Probably only political pressure will bring this about.

In Northern Ireland the Churches are obsessively concerned to maintain their power. It is they who control loyalty; and they jealously guard their sphere of influence. Priests or ministers who fall out of favour with the hierarchies are de facto excommunicated, 'sent to Siberia'. Thus the Church's actions and assertions contradict one another. Theoretically it denies that it has, or wants power. In fact it exercises very considerable power indeed. Education is almost completely dominated by the Churches. The theatre and the arts are under continual pressure. Unable to develop new initiatives of its own, the hierarchy anxiously suppresses those of others. The failing is in the system, not the personally good men who operate it and are obedient to it.

Is the alternative a 'powerless Church', a Church which gladly accepts a servant role in a pluralist society, which frankly identifies itself with the poorest of the poor, and encourages them to think and act for themselves? Seen biblically, such power-lessness, as in Jesus, is anything but ineffective. His power of servanthood overturned the world. It is, however, a very different understanding of power from that of the world around it. A 'people's Church' of this kind would be a very attractive option to some, and is in certain situations probably the only option.

Yet it poses problems. At least for the interim, the priest or minister in basically conservative societies such as Northern Ireland (and Scotland) still wields very considerable power. The people would be lost without such leadership. The Church cannot retreat into an apolitical ghetto. What is needed is more reflection about the proper exercise of power. How can the Church ensure that it uses its influence on behalf of *others*? How can it be trained to shed power, to share power, to divest itself gradually of the trappings of power? How can it move from being a largely clerically-dominated institution?

There are some grounds for optimism. There is questioning within all the Churches. Structures of power and privilege are breaking down, tabus dis-appearing, popular awareness growing — in great part as a result of 'the Troubles'. New initiatives are being launched.

It appears to be a matter of having the wit and the courage to say the right thing at the right time. Leaders who lose the confidence of their followers, who become 'too liberal' can be bumped-off over-night, another reason for extreme caution in being judgmental about individuals in the para-military groups. The members of the latter have been known to develop protection rackets in shops and pubs, with the result that vandalism can sometimes be a highly organised business and the financial stakes can be very high. Many have purely material reasons for wanting a perpetuation of the troubles.

The trouble is that many of the initiatives have been launched by well-meaning outsiders and cut little ice with local people. The activists themselves often want to be 'little Caesars'. It was said (only half-jokingly) that there were nineteen organisations working for peace in Ulster but it was difficult to get them to meet with one another. How could this fragmentation be overcome?

One has to start with people where they are. A whole generation of children has been brought up to regard all law and all discipline with contempt. If they stone the troops who can blame them? The women's nerves have been shot to pieces. If they come out to the street-corner to scream abuse at the army it is because this is preferable to cowering — terrified — in their kitchens.

Thus initiatives can only come from those who know and love the people as they are. Take the example of one small group which, in a difficult area where vandalism and raids by the army made gardening virtually impossible, began to exchange hints and share plants for gardening. This quite genuine base for meeting and common interest developed into a discussion and action group on other community matters, for example the problem of battered wives. As confidence grew visiting speakers were invited to talk on themes from Irish history and in the resultant discussions those of very different political persuasions often found themselves in astonished agreement.

Other groups have had considerable success in establishing relationships across the confessional divide, although in any cross-confessional group there is always the danger that one side would be compromised or even be put in mortal danger if it were known to be meeting with another.

Certainly the most remarkable new initiative from within the Churches has been the lay movement of the Peace People. Catholic and Protestant have linked arms in a spontaneous rejection of continued death and maiming. The outside world, in particular, has seen the Peace People as a hopeful sign of an eventual reconciliation, bringing together people separated by the psychological and cultural barriers of decades, if not centuries. Their marches and community projects have already helped to bring about a less polarised situation. By giving the women-folk a voice, by getting the 'wee wifie' of the side streets to stand up for peace, they have released all manner of new possibilities. Above all, peace has been given something of the romantic flavour and the symbolic colour which had previously been monopolised by the men of violence.

Some of the opposition they have attracted is predictable enough. For example their relatively unpublicised, but highly effective 'life-line' to smuggle out of the country members of the paramilitary groups who want to quit obviously weakens the brutal intimidation of the latter and is correspondingly hated. More worrying, however, is the nature of some of the *support* they have been receiving, the chorus of welcome from the media, the Church hierarchies, the benevolent liberals in arm-chair seclusion.

Hence a less uncritical, though appreciative, approach to the movement is in order. Especially at the beginning, their stress on peace was rather one-sided, and was interpreted by many as meaning peace at any price. Was the long agony of 'the Troubles' to have been in vain? Were the old political bosses to surface again, and take over where they had left off in 1968? This lack of political awareness among the 'Peace People' was not the only criticism. Many felt that they had a strongly middle-class ethos. What had they to say to a com-munity like Ballymurphy, where almost every family had someone interned or jailed, where unemploy-ment ran at thirty-seven per cent, where in an average street five of the men might have been shot?

Yet, particularly for the outsider, it is hard to see how there can be any alternative to a return to the Protestant ascendancy, on the one hand, or to an outright victory for the 'United Ireland' cause, on the other, unless the sort of risks of misunder-standing and one-sidedness run by the Peace People are taken. (Incidents, for example, like the little Catholic child with the placard 'Sorry' on her back in the march up the Shankill, seeming to imply a one-sided repentance.)

What is important is that the Peace People cannot be regarded as a substitute for real political initia-tives. The dreadful scars of 'the Troubles' will never be removed until new political moves are made. For Britain to sit back and applaud the Peace People while keeping the British forces in Northern Ireland is profoundly hypocritical. It demonstrates the bankruptcy not only of our political imagination, but of our moral will, and is a supreme example of our capacity for self-delusion that we imagine that the British forces are an acceptable 'buffer-force'. The brutality and indiscipline of the para-troopers and other British units, accentuated by the rigid class and command structure of the British army, has never been fully appreciated. To spend even a short time in a Republican housing-estate in Belfast is to realise that there is not the slightest possibility of this army 'defusing' the situation. Quite the contrary.

The truth is that the real hate of such communities is directed against 'the Brits', not against the Protestants. The truth is that it is the continued presence of 'the Brits' which maintains the hold of the Provos over the population and gives them a raison d'être. The truth is that nothing is more urgently needed than the rapid, staged withdrawal of the British army and its replacement by a UN peace force.

The argument that British withdrawal will cause a blood-bath, popular among British politicians, owes much to British pride and little to realistic analysis. There are dangers, and they should not be underestimated; but until the army is out of the way the separated communities of Northern Ireland will be unable to come to terms with one another. The fears of a 'blood-bath' are inhibiting the break-through to a new sense of identity, to a better and more just Northern Ireland society.

The present stale-mate, which we are in considerable danger of getting used to, conceals the terrifying possibility of a Hungary-style insurrection, should some incident set the tinder alight again. In the meantime the thankless role of the British army continues, a role which would never be tolerated by the British public if it was a conscript army. We call them professionals, but in fact think of them as mercenaries, doing a job we would never dream of tackling ourselves.

The answer to violence in Northern Ireland can only come from within Northern Ireland. At present it is still very much a 'bunker society', each individual or family defending its own patch. Under the shadow of the British Empire (and the Catholic Empire) little sense of identity, of belonging, of home has been allowed to develop. The last thing it needs today is the crushing paternalism of Westminster or Dublin. Only as it discovers its own independence will solidarity between Catholic and Protestant be cemented, based on a common love of land and people, a common culture and linguistic inheritance, a common passage through innumerable Calvaries. Tomorrow its tribalism can become its pluralism, its divisions its strength.

The best thing we in 'mainland Britain' can do is to worry less about Northern Ireland and learn to love its people and culture more. Certainly our economic investment is necessary, and on a massive scale, but a more sober estimate of what we can contribute and a more generous appreciation of the incredible reserves within Ulster itself is still more needful. Glib pessimism is as dangerous as glib optimism.

When change is experienced as a cancerous growth, the pain felt is expressed in violence. Instead of deploring the violent symptoms the Church must rediscover itself as the advocate and interpreter of change. For the institutional Church this requires as great a revolution in its self-understanding as happened when the Jewish faith was transformed and re-evalued in primitive Christianity. By examining and practising the techniques of peaceful change the Churches can help to alleviate the pain of change. Far more important, they can show that 'the Troubles' are not a destructive cancer but the birth-pangs of the Kingdom, and for that, of course, one needs faith.

In a Belfast kitchen a house Mass is being cele-brated. Outside it is bitter cold. Dogs howl and the army helicopter roars over the roof-tops. The service is reverent but simple — the Gospel read, the prayers spoken by young and old. The bread and wine is shared by Catholic and Protestant. Christ, born and done to death outside the gate, is amongst his people again. Faith is revived again.

Conclusions.
1. Violence in Northern Ireland manifests in ex-treme form structural defects in British society as a whole, not least massive unemployment and class discrimination.
2. The whole terminology of the 'just revolution' appears as inapplicable to the Northern Ireland situation as that of democratic change. Is the Prague Peace Conference's concern for co-existence a more realistic approach?
3. When we talk of violence in Northern Ireland we must include the violence of the British army. It is a myth that it can play a restraining, far less

101

reconciling role, and it should be withdrawn. Other initiatives should be substituted.

4. Judgemental attitudes by the Churches on the para-military movements are counter-productive.

5. The Churches in Northern Ireland will have to question the assumption that their power or influence is necessarily a power or influence for good. For all their pastoral and caritative endeavour the opposite often seems to be the case.

6. The primary contribution of the Churches is to challenge limited loyalties by the larger vision of the Gospel. The prevalence of violence is directly related to this general lack of objectives and orientation.

7. There are hopeful signs amidst the violence and destruction. A new and better Ulster is emerging.

8. There are no convincing theoretical answers to violence in Ulster, only painful and personal ones.

9. If Christians are to do anything at all then non-violence is the only positive option; such non-violence will be risky and should exceed the legally permitted norms of political action.

The Just Revolution

'Germans are only just beginning to discover what free responsibility means. It rests in God, who demands the free, religious risk of responsible action, and who promises forgiveness and consolation to anyone who becomes a sinner because of it.' Dietrich Bonhoeffer

The frontier between violence and non-violence is the critical one for Christian discipleship today, for the exercise of imagination, the development of initiatives, the *doing* of the truth. It is on this frontier that, in the last decade or so, a startling new teaching has begun to spread, that of the 'just revolution'. What are its origins? What is its justification? How does it differ from the previous teachings of the Church on war, peace, and violence?

The traditional doctrine of the 'just war' affirmed the legitimacy of Christian participation in war, in spite of the fact that killing others was regarded as a moral evil, under certain conditions: that it was in a just cause, under legitimate authority, for defined and limited ends, waged by limited means, and when every other alternative had been tried. The medieval view did not, however, authorise rebellion against legitimate authority under any pretext.

At the Reformation, the concept of the 'just war' was grudgingly extended to an act of rebellion against an unjust prince, provided it was led and sanctioned by the preferably unanimous decision of the subordinate political authorities. Luther condemned all violent resistance, even in a just cause, and was particularly allergic to any appeal to the Christian Gospel to justify rebellion. He did, however, eventually affirm the possibility of 'lawful resistance' by the Protestant princes to the Catholic Emperor.

Calvin asserted more explicitly the right of 'minor magistrates' to overturn tyrants. This was put into practice by the Dutch Calvinists and both the French and the Scottish Calvinists developed further his theological legitimation of insurrection, the former in more aristocratic, the latter in more democratic form. This did not amount to a complete sanction of the 'just revolution', since the possibility of a revolution in contemporary terms was not envisaged by sixteenth and seventeenth century political thinkers. It did, however, lead naturally to violent changes in the political régime in England and Scotland.

'Revolution' as we know it today is a new political phenomenon dating from 1789. The understanding of it in political theory was worked out during the 19th and early 20th centuries, notably in the discussion between Marx and the Marxists and Bakunin and the Anarchists. It implies not just a change of political authority, but a complete change of political, social and economic system. The Marxist view, which proved definitive both among the advocates and the opponents of such revolution, sees it as a lengthy historical process. Though it can be hastened or delayed, it is inevitable and total in its effects, and involves at some point the catastrophic use of force for definitive political change.

The use of violence, though normally regarded as inescapable, is for precise and limited ends, and is seen as justified historically, politically and, on certain interpretations of Marx, morally.

Unlike earlier political concepts, the concept of 'revolution' was developed in a secular, often anti-clerical, context. As Marx and others foresaw, it was, like the French Revolution, strongly opposed by the Churches. Both the Marxist and Anarchist theories of revolution were overtaken by events, notably by the October Revolution of 1917, in the light of which Lenin and later Stalin revised Marxist theory, replacing the earlier concept of the 'withering away' of the state by a strengthened concept of 'the dictatorship of the proletariat' (recently rejected by the French Communist Party). As a result, and following historical dynamics already evident in the French Revolution, a greater and more systematic degree of violence was used than was theoretically envisaged.

The Russian Revolution did not have the last word, though it has moulded and hardened anti-revolutionary thinking to a far greater extent than the thinking and practice of later students of Marx and practitioners of Marxist-type revolutions such as Mao Tse-Tung, Ho Chi-Minh, Kwame Nkrumah, or Fidel Castro. Recent historical practice shows that contemporary revolutionaries are often more flexible than their rhetoric would suggest.

The context since the 1950s has increasingly been the Third World, and the relations between Third World countries and the former colonial powers, with more emphasis on economic and social revolution than on political revolution. The inspiration has been nationalist rather than narrowly class-oriented; revolutionary parties have shown marked divergence from the Soviet model and have usually been wider based; the utopian vision and its moral imperative has been dominant. Apart from the recent tragic examples of Ethiopia and Cambodia violence has not been on the same scale as in the USSR (or in contemporary right-wing dictatorships). Furthermore all such revolutions, notably in Africa and Latin America, have been supported by some Christians, usually for clear theological reasons.

Since the World Conference on Church and Society, Geneva 1966, ecumenical discussion on the Christian involvement in revolution has completely changed. In spite of great hesitancy among Western Christians, notably in the UK and West Germany, Christians in the Third World and in Socialist countries have overwhelmingly endorsed the necessity of revolution both in particular countries, and also in the relations between countries (which implies revolution in some sense in the developed world). They have seen this as following the Christian understanding of man, the biblical teaching on justice, and the doctrine of Christian hope.

This does not mean, however, that Third World Christians and those who accept their arguments lightly and thoughtlessly agree that violent means are justified in aiming at a utopian goal. For one thing, violence and revolution are not identical. The prior question, in the view of majority opinion in the ecumenical discussion, is that of revolution. The present world order is unjust and men and women are fighting against this injustice. The Christian Gospel, for its part, contains the vision and promise of a better society and enjoins solidarity with the guilt, suffering and struggle of mankind. Christians can see and must bear witness to the ultimate meaning of this struggle: the reality and possibility of a redeemed community. Commitment to this end realistically implies support and participation in political, social and economic revolution, as also in a revolution in political, ethical and cultural thinking. Christian obedience today, therefore, has revolutionary overtones, not only in 'revolutionary situations' in the Third World, but in our 'democratic situation' in this country. The close international links between different parts of an integrated world system necessitate this.

Secondly, it is necessary to distinguish three ways in which violence occurs in a revolutionary struggle: (1) *primary* violence used by the powers that be as a systematic instrument for maintaining an unjust world order (the extent and sophistication of this has increased alarmingly, and not only in situations of open revolution, for instance in Haiti, South Korea, Indonesia etc.); (2) *secondary* violence of the revolutionaries themselves in protest or resistance to the powers that be and in the conduct of the revolution. Such violence may vary greatly in its extent and nature, but is normally lumped together by defenders of the status quo, who do not distinguish between, for example, sit-down strikes and urban guerilla warfare; (3) *tertiary* violence used by the forces of 'law and order' in suppressing and countering secondary violence, often with unparalleled ferocity and usually with the systematic use of torture. The first and third kinds of violence are not willed by the revolutionary, whose struggle is indeed aimed at their suppression. The attempt to attribute indirect responsibility for tertiary violence to those against whom it is used, denies the traditionally accepted right of self-defence and the right, agreed since the Reformation, of protest and 'lawful resistance' to unjust laws.

Thirdly there are certain things about which Christians involved in this discussion agree and others about which they disagree. They agree (a) that there are some forms of violence which are never justified whatever the end (torture, conquest, deliberate oppression of one group by another); (b) that churches and resistance movements alike have not explored adequately the strategies and effectiveness of non-violence in the struggle for a just society; (c) that non-violence should not be seen as a morally unambiguous, uncontroversial and apolitical form of action, or as one that necessarily excludes others. Multiple strategies are possible. A more sophisticated analysis is required of the nature, implications, effectiveness of violent and non-violent strategies and the reactions which follow from them.

Fourthly, the disagreement among Christians is itself significant, and is not to be seen as a straight disagreement between 'reformist' or 'reactionary' Christians in the West and 'revolutionary' Christians in the Third World or in Socialist countries. Just as some Christians (usually the majority) have accepted the possibility of Christian involvement in a 'just war', and others, usually a small minority, have taken a pacifist position: so with regard to the 'just revolution'. Some Christians in 'revolutionary situations' eschew all politics and take a radically quietist position. The majority, however, are divided into two groups of which the one, possibly in some circumstances the larger group, accepting the concept of a 'just revolution', is ready to participate in it even though this will probably involve the limited use of violence; whereas the other, usually a substantial group, believes that peace and justice cannot be attained by violent means.

Such 'apostles of non-violence' as Martin Luther King and Helder Camara are still *convinced about the need for revolution*, and bear witness to the revolutionary potential and utopian vision of the Christian Gospel. Their 'dream' is not just of a heavenly kingdom; they believe that Christians and other men are bound to work for more peace and justice on earth; they see the hand of God working in contemporary revolutions, even those which use violent means. They are committed to *maintaining solidarity* with their brothers (including Christian brothers) who see themselves inevitably involved in violence. They do not seek, in their personal commitment to non-violent strategies, to keep themselves free from the stain of sin. Rather they believe that the Christian witness is to use means which are fully consistent with the end desired, in order to ensure that the new society is indeed new and not just the substitution of one ruling group for another. In some cases, their non-violence is a provisional option, and represents the conviction that violence can only legitimately be used as a last resort, and that non-violent options are still open, and have rarely been used in a large and systematic scale.

The alternative view of revolutionary Christians who are prepared, in the extreme case, to sanction the use of violence for a just revolution is represented by various writers such as Camillo Torres, Richard Shaull, James Cone and others; it is an option adopted by such contemporary Christians as Abel Muzorewa, Robert Mugabe, Julius Nyerere, Kenneth Kaunda and other leaders in Southern

Africa today. Those who take this position believe that their primary task is to work for a better society in certain precise and attainable ways, and that the use of violence in strictly limited and controlled ways is necessary to attain this society, and to end an unjust and violent situation. They do not maintain that this is the only Christian path, or that violence is always justified, nor do they forget the inevitable ambiguity of violent action, and the difficulty in practice of limiting it or restraining it.

It is important to note that these two options, far from representing extreme positions, are in some ways much closer to each other than the earlier 'pacifist' and 'just war' positions. This is true *ethically*, in the sense that neither view is indifferent to the moral imperative of the struggle for justice, nor to the moral problem which the possibility of taking human life inevitably raises. In neither case is the ethical responsibility of the individual Christian removed by the simple application of a general moral law. It is true *politically* in that supporters of both positions can work together and respect each other's stand.

In this way the double standards of the medieval position (one law for the Christian layman and another for the cleric) are avoided. So, too, is the polarisation characteristic of modern times when pacifist and non-pacifist have rejected each other's positions and sought to show that they were illogical or unChristian. Rather the emphasis is placed on the *positive* aspects of each position. The divide is not an absolute one. The pacifist and the non-pacifist committed to the struggle for a just future regard one another, on most issues, as allies. The pacifist respects the stance of the non-pacifist as a possible, and conscientiously held alternative, and vice-versa. The confessional chasm no longer lies between pacifist and non-pacifist but between those on the side of liberation and those who supported the oppressive structures of the status quo. It is the latter which is, for the Christian, the *impossible* alternative today.

This is not to play down, in any way, the continuing and crucial importance of the question whether or not the use of violence by the Christian is permissible or even necessary. Quite the contrary. Only where this question is a real one is Christian discipleship being taken seriously. A pacifist unperturbed by the failure of non-violence to change the South African situation has as little credibility as the non-pacifist who refuses to face up to the total impasse created by violence in the Ulster situation.

South Africa poses the dilemma in its cruellest form for the pacifist. It is a land which has been Christianised for a hundred years, and where the blacks have been politically organised for more than sixty years. Despite the incredible exploitation and humiliation they have suffered at the hand of the white man they are still anxious to create a multi-racial society once change has been effected.

Yet at the moment, despite decades of struggle to bring about change by constitutional and non-violent means, the clock is actually being put back in terms of their social and political rights. Increasingly they are turning to violence as the only hope of change. Can we, particularly we in the West, blame them? Have we a moral foot to stand on if we urge them to be 'patient'? Does not a comfortable complacency give the lie to our alleged humanitarian concern about a 'blood-bath'?

There is still 'naught for our comfort' in South Africa, and the dilemma is equally cruel for the non-pacifist. Violence, once resorted to, would almost certainly perpetuate itself, and the attempt to keep it 'strictly limited and controlled' would be subject to the caveat that such limits would be observed as long as victory could be gained by them, and no longer. Above all, however, the rhetoric of liberation violence would have to come to terms with the formidable military power of the South African government, which between 1963 and 1973 spent more on arms than all other African nations combined, and is now manufacturing napalm and nerve gas. Of its will to fight there need be no doubt. To topple it violently a massive reliance on foreign intervention will probably be necessary, with all the consequent implications for internal change and world peace.

It may be that the evidence we have as to the efficacy of violence or non-violence remains ambiguous. We in Britain should be very cautious indeed about too confident pronouncements on the subject, but infinitely less cautious in our solidarity with those actually involved in the struggle for peace and justice in South Africa. Why has so little attention been paid to encouraging South African *whites* to take the costly path of conscientious objection? Why has so little progress been made in imposing effective economic sanctions on South Africa, whose Achilles heel is its reliance on heavy European investment? If a perpetuation of the present régime and a resort to bloody confrontation are both

equally unthinkable have we not a peculiar responsibility to exercise all the leverage we can before
it is too late? A revolution in our attitude is required
here, if we are to purge ourselves of the old 'kith
and kin' mentality, a still more painful revolution in
the attitudes of the white South Africans. Only a
miracle could accomplish such changes, but the fact
is that all the alternatives to such a miracle hap-
pening are *too appalling to contemplate*.

What, then, is our distinctive witness as Christians in the struggle, whether violent or non-violent,
for a more humane world? What does it mean to be
a Christian revolutionary? Often the initiative will
not be in our hands, whether in South Africa or
elsewhere. How does the ultimate loyalty of the
Christian shape his actions and his aspirations?
Many contemporary Christians from the Third
World point to the need to criticise the revolution
from within lest it become institutionalised in structures as oppressive as those they replace. Others urge
the development of a 'spirituality of liberation' to
enable the Christian community to keep one step
ahead of the revolution.

There is a need, too, to see things in their relation
to *all* humanity. Do those, for example, who reluc-
tantly accept the necessity for armed revolution in
Southern Africa want to say the same about countries in Eastern Europe where human rights are
oppressed? If not, why not? In the last resort, is it a
theological or a political commitment we are
making? Does a Marxist analysis underpin the
support of violent revolution in the Third World?
Conversely, does an outdated theology of the State
explain why the average Western church-goer

accepts the necessity of an army but rejects that of revolution?

Not the least of the advantages of a new spirituality of liberation would be a rigorous and honest analysis of our own mixed motives in such questions, to disentangle our different loyalties, and to see where we are being Christian and where 'merely British'.

The 'discerning of the spirits' will not be easy. Both peace and justice can become abstract principles, obstacles to realism and humanity. The Prague Peace Conference, with its passionate concern for peaceful co-existence, has to be kept in mind as firmly as the clarion calls of the Third World churches for revolutionary change.

Compassion has to be yoked to realism, not the easy realism of the cynic, but one based on careful analysis, on stringent tests of feasibility, on openness to all available evidence. The revolutionary solution may, for example, be applicable only in relatively straightforward situations. The more complex the social structures — such as those in Ulster or Lebanon — the less chance there seems to be that any sort of resolution to the conflict will be secured by revolutionary action, violent or non-violent.

In some situations, such as South Africa, a many-pronged approach may be advisable, gradualist and revolutionary tactics being pursued simultaneously, with the long-term aim of bringing about a radical change in the patterns of political and economic power. Given the political developments in Africa as a whole such a change is, in the long run, inevitable. Black South Africans now know this, and so, in their hearts, do the whites. The tide runs strongly, it may be irresistibly, towards awesome violence.

If this appals us, we will have to improve on our present performance, deploring apartheid verbally, but economically and to an extent politically reaching it a life-line; hoping for a peaceful solution, but unable to envisage the Anglo-Afrikaner minority willingly abandoning their power and privilege. No wonder neither side respects us. Our supposed *via media* rests on a quicksand.

Somehow the British churches have to convey to the 'great British public' the realisation that the only alternative to a frank support of the present régime is commitment to revolutionary change in South Africa, not as a sell-out of our peace witness, but as the last chance of ensuring any lasting peace there.

Conclusions

1. Within the British Churches there has been a considerable shift in attitudes to war and revolution.

2. On the one hand, the pacifist case receives at least a courteous hearing. Many factors explain this willingness to listen to the pacifist case, not least the loss of Britain's imperial role, the development of nuclear weapons, the need to co-exist with Communism.

3. On the other hand, concern for the Third World, often spear-headed by representatives of Britain's missionary tradition, and reinforced by contacts at Vatican or WCC level, has nudged many in the direction of a theology of revolution.

4. The result is that both traditional just war theories and a pacifism unconcerned with social

change are increasingly discredited.

5. A certain continuity exists between the just war and the just revolution arguments, a continuity which the most radical pacifist cannot overlook, above all the ultimate readiness to use force.

6. However, the overwhelming positive concerns of the just revolution theory constrain the pacifist to react with his own positive alternatives and initiatives.

7. There is a growing area of pragmatic discussion about appropriate means of facilitating change between pacifist and non-pacifist. Pathos and rhetoric are at a discount on both sides.

8. The great majority of church-goers in Britain are virtually untouched by this debate. This is the untypical aspect of the West European situation.

9. To 'bring the situation home' a new symbolism is needed to engage the imagination (cf. ch. 8), and the arguments must be related to the acute question of violence within UK (ch. 6), to particular and local situations. (ch. 9).

Pointers Beyond Death

'Noticing in the distance a fig-tree in leaf, Jesus went to see if he could find anything on it. But when he came there he found nothing but leaves; for it was not the season for figs. He said to the tree "May no one ever again eat fruit from you."'
Mark 11, 12f

Nothing is expected from the Church except the impossible. It is to bear figs in spring, to anticipate the harvest of the Kingdom, to liberate in the face of death. Its language is lyrical, absurd, folly to the wise. The runes of liberation point beyond death, but in the language of song and symbol, sign and story, seed and fig-tree. They stir and enlarge the imagination by the poetic dream.

For we have to grope our way forward, step by step, seizing on symbols, relating experience as parable, generating energy for the future by 'telling stories' from the past. We cannot wait indefinitely for some fullness of vision, or bruise the complexities of reality to fit into the rigidities of our little systems. How shall we *talk* about the future society we dream of and work for? Not in the computerised projections of the futurologist, not in the pre-packaged remedies of the social engineer. It is the creative symbol that we respond to, for it alone spins us out of our accustomed orbits and propels us towards the genuinely new.

Side by side with the impatient activist, shunning death, and the docile quietist who is obsessed by it, there is room for the gentle revolutionary, the Francis of Assisi, the mystic, the clown, the lover, who juggles reality into new forms, for whom death is 'our sister', who talks this other language.

Our perception of reality is so strait-laced, hide-bound, plodding. In our conflicts and controversies what we often need more than anything else is to catch a glimpse of our wearyingly familiar situation from an unexpected angle, so that it is shaken out, opened up, trans-valued. This is the charisma of the genuine peace-maker, that he can offer an imaginative re-evaluation of a situation which eases folk out of the clinch they have got into. The symbol, the parable, the liturgical celebration can do this, flipping a too tidy mind into actual thought, recharging the batteries of wonder or expectation.

One of the unexpected by-products of this project on the just peace was the comparison between the styles of the different groups.

Edinburgh, on the whole, kept all extravagances of emotion at a proper distance. It was at its happiest analysing or pursuing the elusive thread of a cogent argument. It buttressed itself with clauses, conclusions and qualifications to conclusions. Belfast, on the other hand, was less easy to pin down. Bemused visitors to its meetings were exposed to avalanches of anecdotes and delphic utterances with no immediately apparent logical connections. Its aversion to the jargon of intellectuals was, however, phrased in pellucid terms.

What *is* the appropriate discourse for a theology of justice and peace? How far can we use 'manageable' language to express our deepest longings, our fears of the void and nothingness?

Theology's job to put things into the most total context available. If it is talking about man, for example, it must not restrict itself to genes and glands, though it must also be interested in those. It must speak also about the interaction of people who relate to one another and create one another in freedom. If it is talking about politics, it cannot just talk of the various ends which men and women desire. It must talk of the limits of human capacity, and perhaps of their overcoming.

The most serious of these limits is death. Not only does death bring to an obvious end the political aspirations of individuals and communities; the realisation of political ends *involves* death. To have a 'polis', a community of citizens, involves the definition of disruptive activity which cannot be tolerated or incorporated. The 'treatment' of offenders may not, technically, involve their deaths, though if 'life' or 'death' have qualitative overtones and are not mere biological terms, any violation of freedom such as imprisonment, or forced re-education tends to death. Whether it is in terms of what our middle-class existence costs a council housing-estate like Easterhouse, or our British existence costs the Third World, or the Cultural Revolution costs the Revisionist opponents, it seems built into the structures of our existence that we create death as well as being its victims.

In the face of this perception, what can political hope *mean*? A kind of stoical heroism, banging one's head against a brick wall, in the hope that a few people will be morally infected enough to live against their instincts, and to surrender their own lives, or a bit of them, for the sake of their neighbour's? Or a steady recognition that even a little improvement in the present distribution is worth plugging away at — and that the big question of

119

death is just a distraction? Should we just get on managing the manageable?

Obviously man *is* a social being. Without the educational, vocational, recreational opportunities provided by society he cannot even begin to exist, to be himself. The exclusion of social ends also involves death. The only way to love one's neighbour is through politics.

What is being argued here, however, is that death, as the ultimate menace to community, sets the sharpest of limits to all political aspiration. If man is to be liberated, even in the face of death, it will not be by new social orders, however just and humane. The christian activist, who sometimes seems to put all his eggs in the political basket, needs to be reminded of this. Imagining he is taking Christianity into politics, he can gradually leave it behind in order to be whole-hearted in his political commitment. This is not to say that politicians should be paralysed by their limitations, but that they should not confuse their pragmatically demanded compromises with acting for the Kingdom of God. As Christian political activity it will be constantly, and perhaps creatively, aware of its distance from the conditions of the Kingdom.

The political process as such is not invalidated by such limitations. After all, as the Habitat Conference showed, a significant area of human endeavour can and should be 'managed'. The basic problem is to find the will and the means to forge ahead in spite of the frustration by human selfishness. In each situation the problem of integrity is posed anew. At what point does the responsible compromise between the possible and the perfect drift into mere expediency?

In political terms, for example, what does it mean to 'love one's enemy'? It is difficult to envisage concrete situations which carry that meaning. An incident was described from Czechoslavakia in which an inspecting Party official, resigned in advance to the inevitable hostility he would meet, received instead a spontaneous word of sympathy for his difficult task. This completely nonplussed him and led to a remarkably open discussion. Such opportunities are seldom perceived because political self-identification by any group usually necessitates an enemy, someone whose presence one would rather be without, a kind of will-to-death, even if we are too civilised to act on it.

It is the person thrown up by the system at any particular time that one must engage with. What one loves one must aim to preserve, not destroy. This, of course, applies only to the personality of the opponent, and not to the system which he represents. The Christian way puts us into the thick of politics. We are bound to stand up to our opponents and thus to have enemies. Somehow, however, we must understand them better than they do themselves, see them as they 'really' are, not put *ourselves* in their way but the chance of a better being for themselves. This involves self-control and self-criticism. Loving, instead of hating, means changing oneself, and thus anticipating, in the new personal relationship, the hoped-for change in the whole political system.

A key problem is the general atrophy of imagination. Our 'natural' range of sympathies seems limited indeed. Changes in local traffic regulations, for example, can arouse the most intense and sustained public indignation, but these same friendly and generous (and indignant) people react with indifference or resignation to the crucial issues of war and peace, over-population, world hunger and so on. It is obvious that moralising is of no avail. How can we bring the really serious issues within the compass of people's imagination?

People do have a rare capacity for dying for those they love, but such love can rarely be generalised to causes, communities or the general welfare of mankind. Only when those are focussed in specific people do they tend to come alive. Indeed the particularity and exclusiveness of our loves usually means that, faced with the crunch, we would naturally let the other child die for our child, or will that, given, say, one kidney machine and two children. It is doubtful if this is a matter for moralising. It seems to be our nature.

The Gospel affirms that we can grow into a second nature — not by screwing ourselves up to it morally, but by some kind of involvement with the life of Christ or God which changes us. Occasionally we detect quite concrete instances of the 'transforming', which are *not* a matter of moral effort in those concerned: people who have found that their freedom and their 'being-for' someone else converge instead of diverging.

The Church, at its best, is a symbolic image of this 'involvement with the life of God', of this larger generosity. Sadly the central image of communion, through death, into life, is so mocked by the empirical existence of the churches in their life preservation, and by the lack of expressed tension between symbol and fact, that it almost loses credence at all.

A symbol, once established, whether a word, a name, a slogan or a ritual, can present a whole complex of issues in a flash. It can arouse a wide array of emotionally charged associations without further appeal to rational or other considerations. It can be a powerful cohesive force.

In liturgy, for example, a ritual act can gather into itself a whole world of meaning. The symbol lives as long as there are people dedicated to what it represents. It can develop additional depth and meaning from its repetition in different social milieux. We must hold on to the tradition till something better arrives to replace it.

The difficulty is that much of the Church's symbolism has died or gone slack, so that it no longer prods the imagination into play against the facticity of our present existence. In our public and social life today new symbols are needed to give our society a sense of direction, to capture the imagination for the grand issues of the day. We no longer inhabit the same world as our forefathers. Their symbols are no longer adequate. Yet creating symbols, thinking them up, is inclined to be disastrous. They should emerge naturally, 'grow out of the earth'. For African theologians, for example, the Exodus, the setting free of the people of Israel, has a powerful significance as a symbol of liberation. Artists, poets, musicians can contribute here, but art is largely cut off from religion. The Church is isolated from all the best sources of symbolic life.

In relation to politics it would be important for the Church's symbolism to express that what is unmanageable about man — his love, his freedom, his death — is more crucial to his identity than what is manageable about him: his instincts for self-preservation, his material needs, his organisability. It should find room for his dreams and fantasy, help him to articulate the longings which are so often repressed and hidden.

The 'transformed' community of the Church should stand symbolically against all forms of natural selectivity, in terms of wealth, origin, status. It should, that is, be 'catholic' not sectarian in principle, though in practice quite intelligible social or psychological reasons may prevent it achieving anything like catholicity.

In its symbolism, the present raggedness and limitedness of the community's faithfulness should be set against the 'vision of the Kingdom', the source of its restlessness, its dissatisfaction with things as they are, but also of hope.

A symbol is not just a pointer to the beyond. It registers one's present distance from Jerusalem, from Utopia, from the far country where death is no more. This tension has to be sustained. In its political actions the Church has three options:

It may, at worse, be sheerly hypocritical, identifying its own institutional interests and the personal welfare of its individual members with the cause of the Kingdom.

It may compromise with the world, taking some thought for the morrow, stewarding the power given it, fencing itself around with a degree of privilege, but it would do so in constant horror at the bondage it shares with the world. Its central tension would remain the world's need to be freed, its central celebration the hope that we are 'on the way'.

Or it may refuse to compromise, live in the 'style of the Kingdom', and, since the world is still in the grip of death, be crucified.

The second and third options are both types of faithfulness, both witnessing by putting a symbolic question mark against various political expediencies. It is not, of course, always easy to distinguish the second from the first, but it may well be that this symbolic being and action is the most important contribution which the Church has to make in the political realm. If we cannot make bread out of stones, and refuse to insult our neighbour by offering him stones *instead* of bread, we can at least ensure that the very stones cry out at its absence.

Conclusions.

1. Symbols are pointers to the unmanageable in life.
2. Our whole culture is drenched with Christian symbolism, reflecting the role of Christianity in our tradition.
3. We are virtually immunised against much of this symbolism. It seldom has the power to move us.
4. Banal and materialist symbols have flooded in to fill this vacuum, as the world of advertisement shows.
5. Symbols emerge on certain frontiers, between past and present, life and death, power and powerlessness. We cannot contrive them.
6. A too tightly programmed theology has no room for symbols; their absence should always be seen as a warning.
7. A too tightly programmed ethic has no room for imaginative re-evaluation; it excludes spontaneity

and risk.

8. The alternative to violence may be in spontaneous, caring actions which put others 'off their guard', 'revalue' them in their own eyes and in ours.

Life-Style

> 'Do all the parts of your duty as earnestly as if the salvation of all the world and the whole glory of God, and the confusion of all devils, and all that you hope or desire, did depend upon every one action.' Jeremy Taylor

The concern about life-style, in its present form at least, is a relatively new one. It reflects a growing awareness both of the inequity of the distribution of the world's wealth and of the finite nature of the world's resources. Radicals, conservationists, and counter-cultural elements jog along side by side here. What is common to all is the *practical* thrust, the weariness with mere talk, the determination to do something, however small, to bring one's life into line with one's conscience. In its way it represents a quiet revolution, an attractively non-violent way of facing up to the obscene contrast between our affluence and the deprivation of the Third and Fourth Worlds.

The aim of this chapter is to relate these very promising initiatives to the wider concern for peace and justice. So often thinking about the 'alternative society' tends to side-step the wider problems of society and politics and to concentrate on individual patterns of consumption or use of energy. The 'drop-out' solution is, however, no solution — at least for the great majority. Equally unsatisfactory, on the other hand, are the recommendations, admirable in themselves, to grow one's own vegetables, ride a bicycle to work, and so on. At best these are symbolic, at worst trivial gestures. We need the sort of critique of authoritarian and unjust structures in society as a whole offered by liberation theology to give us a framework within which the perplexed individual, weighed down by family, house and insurances, can take a broader view of the situation.

For the individual and the group the hope of a more authentic humanity lies not only in his or her personal life-style but in developing, as it were in the interstices of society, ever more co-operative and participatory groupings as a base from which to reform those structures which inhibit us. By focusing on the social sin involved in these structures liberation theology gives us a practical weapon against the numbing and pervasive sense of powerlessness in the face of evil.

In a society where an impersonal complex of bureaucracy and technology, of social and political and economic factors, seems to determine virtually everything, and where the individual seems dwarfed and futile and powerless, the peculiar Christian contribution may well be to inject this note of hope. Over these powers too the Cross has vanquished. Believing this we can put our mind to humanising a process which otherwise threatens to engulf us.

We face, then, as much a challenge to the imagination as to the conscience, a challenge to experiment in a hundred different ways, to resist the packaged values of consumerism by enriching the quality of life. For some this means, in individual terms, if not a wholly vegetarian diet, at least the reduction of meat consumption to one or two meals a week. The more meat there is on our table, the less staple diet in the form of grain there will be in someone else's food bowl. We must all resist the frantic pursuit of possessions, the encouragement of waste. Do we allow other people to borrow our car or is it a sacred possession?

Behind such particular suggestions and questions lies the quest for a distinctive Christian life-style, marked by the openness, the sharing, the vulnerability of the Cross, one which should be visible in the institutional church as well as in individuals. We have to ask whether the present structures of the Church truly reflect a will to renew our life-style.

Some specific examples of areas for experimentation were explored by the London group and may prove suggestive for others. They are not meant to be prescriptive and are quite certainly not exhaustive.

Take, for example, the question of *Housing*. Humanly speaking, the house provides both shelter and 'controlled space'. We need it not only for protection from the weather but also as an 'arena of living', in which we can have some control over our own existence and which can be an expression of our personality, a symbol of our community, a miniature of our world.

Sadly, many people are denied this by the present mal-distribution of house space. Only public action can put this right, but voluntary initiative can pave the way, for example, by the amalgamation of households, or by the enlargement of households through the kind of hospitality that becomes so permanent that it transcends hospitality.

This may be seen as an infringement of privacy. The aim is in fact to enlarge freedom, to enable people to choose their own style of household and to create their own environment. Public control of the *allocation* of space would be in the interests of the private control of the *use* of it.

Instead of the present system for the construction, equipment and adornment of houses which presents the user with finished products and which encourages a 'cult of competitive uniformity', people might be provided with no more than a 'shelter shell' which they could then shape, construct, equip according to their own tastes.

Or take the closely related issue of the *family*. In practice we are being squeezed between an increasingly institutionalised society and a tense and unsupported nuclear family, Mum and Dad and their one, two, or three children. Given such a limited variety of relationships folk in our urban conglomerations are just unable to cope. It is not only ecological considerations about the need to pool resources but a new awareness of liberating, loving relationships which requires a radical revision of the traditional stereotypes of family life.

The large majority will continue to prefer the nuclear family base, but something of the intolerable weight put on it can be taken off by food-co-operatives, baby-sitting circles, whatever helps people to develop their own gifts and humanity. The whole pattern of expectation has to be changed, and the trend towards the professionalisation and institutionalisation of society (welfare services) resisted, a trend common to capitalist and communist countries. Incoherent structures are created which develop their own momentum, and within which virtually no one has control or responsibility.

This raises the question of *Church communities*.

The presuppositions of British society are through and through individualistic. Our survival and success has depended upon the impression we give of competence, adequacy, and self-sufficiency. These laudable, but one-sided virtues have made our family life every bit as brittle and power-obsessed as our professional life is.

The same is true of our Church life. The Bible expects us to be candid, open, and vulnerable (Eph. 4:15). Not only are we very far from being this community of honesty, our churches today are far more divided by property and possessions than were those of the early Christians (Acts 4:32-5; Heb. 13: 16; 1 John 3:16-18).

The Church is there to be the working exhibit of God's way on earth. Increasing numbers are responding to this by committing themselves to alternative forms of life-style, especially to life in intentional communities which minister to the needy, express solidarity with the oppressed and develop close fellowship with others in a depersonalized world. There is now enough experience to confirm that this is a uniquely viable form of living for Christians in the waning years of the twentieth century.

These specific examples point to the emergence of a (still very loose) consensus about the evolution of new patterns of relationship, patterns more appropriate to a Christianity which is 'come of age'. The main themes of this consensus can be summarised as follows:

1. *Participation*

The championing of 'participation' seems to have

two elements. It is a plea for more equal relationships, and this egalitarian concern expresses itself in
a suspicion of dominance and hegemony of all kinds
— political and professional. It is also a plea for
'organic' rather than 'mechanical' relations, i.e.
more living, unitive or sharing relations between
people and with nature.

2. *Simplicity*

Caution is in order here. With what is simplicity
being contrasted? With complexity or with incoherence? Sometimes it is complexity that is opposed,
but others who plead for simplicity welcome complexity, as Teilhard de Chardin did. Their worry is
with incoherence. For some the plea for simplicity
— and smallness — represents a rejection of technology and efficiency; for others it represents a
desire for greater efficiency and better technology.

3. *Community*

The new stress on community and co-operation is
as much opposed to collectivism as to individualism,
to the cult of the public in state socialism as to the
privatisation of life. The call for 'community' sometimes represents a quarrel with private property,
private consumption and the nuclear family, and
sometimes with the dominant state and the powerful public corporations. Elements in early socialism
are being rediscovered here. One significant development is that consumer co-operatives are now
being complemented by housing and producer co-
operatives.

4. A 'General Worry about Things'

The worry about consumerism, acquisitiveness, waste and pollution is very diffuse and needs careful analysis. It seems to have three elements — an economic or ecological concern about what people do to *things*, a psychological or spiritual concern about what the possession and consumption of things do to *people*, and a social or interpersonal concern about what the distribution of things does to people's *relationships*.

How all these concerns relate to the question of violence or to Christian affirmations is not clear. But one thing *is* clear:

5. *There is a close relation between poverty and war.*

Their internal dynamics are similar. The gut or inner reality of both is the rejection and violation of people. In that sense, poverty is war in slow motion, a mild form of killing and maiming. For poverty is *impoverishment*, not something that just happens to people, a mere state of affairs, but something that people do to each other, a human interaction, a social pattern — of people rejecting and violating people.

The argument here is not that poverty causes war, which is as may be, but that poverty does to people what war does, only less intensely, clearly and brutally. It could be said to do so in four ways.

It *reduces* or dishonours them; they are 'done down'.

It *arrests* or inhibits their growth; they are 'done in'.

It *removes* or distances them; they are 'done away'.

It *deprives* them of life resources; they are 'done'.

Poverty in this sense is a main mark, a pervasive and determinative structural feature of British society today. The most stable form of this poverty is the social pattern of graded power which we call *class*. For it is principally across the lines of graded power that rejection takes place. Economic power over things and social power over people are intimately linked. There can be no room for complacency about the high degree of human violation in our society due to this twofold pattern of poverty and class. Hence a less violent style of life must mean less poverty, less class. Mere changes in *consumption* will not affect this, and it is not enough for 'life style' groups to concentrate on how we consume and spend while forgetting about how we produce and earn.

Over the last half century the structure of society has changed remarkably little. At the top a small group still possesses immense wealth. In industry the concentration of power is increasing. Less than 100 firms produce fifty per cent of manufactured goods. At the other end there is a large group entirely dependent on selling their labour in a market controlled by the small property group. Workers' conditions and wages have improved, but policy decisions remain the privilege of the few. The so-called managerial group is exceedingly hard to distinguish in practice from the proprietorial group. How then, is change to be encouraged? Unless both the deep existential factors and the broad institutional ones are tackled, the life-style question will be trivialised. Already it has been interpreted as a case of the middle class belittling consumption now that the working class is on to it, or as a prudential policy of saving up for future consumption, or as yet another example of Christian self-directed aggression, welcomed by vested interests as a distraction from analysis.

The problem is a mammoth one. We have to work simultaneously at the psychological structures of self-rejection and other-rejection and at the social structures of political and economic exclusion.

The crux of the latter may be the *rights of control* over the factors of *large-scale production* for *exchange*. Would it be better if exchange were less dominant? If large scale production were less prevalent? If rights of control were less concentrated? Do these offer points of leverage towards a less violent, less impoverished, less enclassed structure and style of life?

How far will the attempt to move towards a less violent, participatory life-style tend actually to provoke conflict, if not violence? It seems inevitable that any attempt to bring 'bits of the Kingdom of Heaven into the present' will arouse hostility. It may help to have more people trained in non-violent methods made available to groups trying to change situations, e.g. by the use of squatting.

Take the case of R.F. McKenzie, the headmaster of Summerhill Academy who sought to abolish corporal punishment and to give special attention to disadvantaged children. Despite support from many of his teachers and an education committee which

135

was generally progressive, his initiatives led to a mounting campaign of verbal violence which led to his dismissal. Indeed the outcome for Scotland as a whole seems to have been negative — a reaction against liberal trends. If the only answer is a long-term strategy, what happens in the meantime to the parents, children and teachers involved?

In the view of the majority of British Christians, of course, the 'system' had to be supported in such situations to prevent violence erupting. How can change be brought about without appearing to threaten all order? It is important that we work at two levels simultaneously, not only moving into the power structures, but engaging in genuine community self-analysis to prevent sterile and mechanical confrontation. We should have high hopes of changing the situation. In the good news about humanity Christians have reason to hope.

In practice, it is often difficult to decide which role one is playing when working within an institution and hoping to change it. In order to 'get things done' is it not legitimate and necessary at times to play the political power game? Yet, at the same time, one is dealing with people. Are the personal relationships with them simply to be sacrificed 'for the cause'?

The recognition of the fragmentariness of all progress in humanising society should be a safeguard against the temptation to programme people along puritanical and rigorist lines, to 'use' them. There is no one magic solution to society's ills. It would be high irony indeed if, in our concern to 'advance' society, we were to adopt the tactics of the commissar. The ever more urgent task is to reinforce the human rights of the individual, or of the grass-roots community, over against the planner. It is a mistake always to be pursuing tangible results. People have a miraculous ability to survive through and despite the system and keep their humanity.

Our perception, too, of the way in which important changes happen is often at fault. In a hollow way outdated structures can linger on for decades. The important thing is, say, how the Dubcek episode in Czechoslovakia will look like in twenty, fifty, one hundred years time. For the individual the difficulty is how to keep plugging away in an apparently adverse situation. One thing is sure. The eventual course of events will never be in line with one's expectations.

In contemporary Britain gains can be recorded in all sorts of specific areas, greater humanity in the schools, for example, better provision for the unemployed. But hope and hopelessness cannot be quantified, weighed up mathematically in this way. Do sociological factors alone explain why there are such armies of the apathetic for each hopeful individual? How pathetic the latter's attempts to communicate seem to be compared with the destruction wreaked by the violent and the hopeless!

Certainly realism is in place here. There can be no glib complacency about the victory of good over evil, no updated version of the 'theology of glory' so beloved by establishment churches. The churches themselves have a miserable track record in freeing men from the fear of sin, of guilt, of evil, as anti-semitism, the witch-craze, and heresy-hunts show — all attempts to project onto others our sense of inadequacy in the face of evil. At our peril do we try to 'explain away' evil. In its inscrutability it deserves almost the same reverence as the Good. The power of evil is all too clear.

What began as a very down to earth discussion on life-style turns, of necessity, to these ultimate questions.

How do we explain the universal sense of bondage? Like 'Honest Iago', never allowed to forget his origins, to escape his past, we seem to be caught in a hopeless situation, the only compensation for our self-hurt as we flail around being that we too can inflict pain on others, caught like the fly in the glue-bottle.

Or should we regard evil as the imposter, the pretender, the yawning gap between where we are and what we are created for? Has it really any meaning or substance in itself? Is it not always a limitation, a falling short of the mark, of the positive goal we are set? Is not oppression the outcome of arrested development? Because growth, becoming, achieving, true self-hood is so painful and difficult we develop techniques to evade it. We settle for a lesser identity. We keep people at a distance, for only after having done this can we be heartless enough to deprive, oppress them. Conversely, it is this very distance which makes it necessary for us to exploit them, as compensation for the loss in human contact. The undeniable horrors and cruelties of life appear to be the price exacted by the human experiment, by the long process of development. No one ever knowingly 'chooses the devil'. We choose what it seems we are made for.

The challenge is to *understand* why some want to dominate, and why others want to be dominated.

There is no ultimate absurdity here. We must see behind the conflict of power and the clash of interests to this *deeper dynamic*. Only as we train ourselves in such identification will we be able to show the conflicting parties that, in the end of the day their interests are identical.

Worship should be a training in such discernment and identification. We must ask the question of liberation in respect of worship. Too often the assumption behind so much of our conventional worship is that we have to learn to reconcile ourselves to failure, to accommodate ourselves. What is needed is a close and concrete 'exercise' which involves us in our situation but in a different mode, which trains us to see it and ourselves differently.

We need a 'spirituality of achievement'. We need to be disciplined for the rigours of decisive action, trained to see our little world in the light of the whole drama of redemption. This rediscovery of the Bible and of the liturgy as a celebration of liberation may allow the heroic dimensions of discipleship to surface again in our own time.

In all our *relationships* self-knowledge is imperative. We have to be aware of the destructive quality of criticism, of branding others as complete failures unless they follow one particular way. The more open the relationship the more charity is needed, for the closer we are, the more vulnerable we become. One's identity is at risk. The fashionable enthusiasm for openness has its pitfalls. It is false to imagine that open relationships can lead to absolute honesty, complete self-knowledge. Progress will be relative.

Violence. Here, too, we should be cautious of

thinking in too absolute terms. Instead of non-violence (who is ever completely non-violent?), should we be talking of 'less violence'? Should we retitle the project, 'Less violence, more justice, and a little bit of peace!!'

This is not to open the flood-gates to an easy relativism. It is, however, all too easy to feel overwhelmed by the so manifest failure to achieve a better world if our criteria are too absolute. What has all the dedicated effort of so many good men and women availed? By absolute standards, perhaps very little.

Yet we should remember the positive influence of all those involved in the struggle for a better order. Their numbers are certainly greater than ever before. The world-wide waves of protest against injustice in our own time have been interpreted by some as evidence of an extraordinary ethical revival. Who has a long enough perspective to be able to evaluate all this correctly? The Human Rights movement in the Eastern bloc is a new and positive development. Our gloom in the West is not shared by those we account most oppressed; by, for example, the blacks in South Africa. This courage to try, and to keep on trying, is often under-pinned by the Christian hope.

It is hard, then, to see the theology of hope, of liberation as reductionist, or provincial, or unspiritual. Quite the opposite. It has many variants. In South America, for example, there are Protestant and Pentecostalist varieties as well as Catholic ones, 'orthodox' and less 'orthodox' ones. It is, above all, a method, a way of doing theology, which relates directly to practice, to life-style. At every point the key question it asks is whether what is being said and done furthers liberation or domination. Unless we want the British churches to become reductionist, provincial and unspiritual it is this indirect application which we should be pursuing in our British context.

Conclusions

1. There is a direct, causative relation between our way of living and world justice. The standard of living 'we' demand presupposes the political and economic oppression of the 'Third World', as we see most vividly in our white brothers in South Africa.

2. There is nothing wrong with material wealth as such, with technology as such, with enjoying all good things of life.

3. The aim of liberation movements is to overcome poverty, not to embrace it.

4. Care should be taken that a specifically 'Christian' life-style does not lead to legalism or 'churchiness'.

5. None of us can ever do anything *for* others. We can only enlarge their freedom to act for themselves. Those we imagine we can 'help' may well be those from whom we have to start learning.

6. Unemployment of quite unacceptable proportions, housing deprivation, and racial discrimination are among the factors creating a growing number of alienated ghetto communities, which see little future for themselves in our society.

7. Intolerable conditions of poverty and dehumanisation will not be resolved without conflict

and suffering.

8. We should not assume too quickly that our task is to work for the integration of the impoverished into our national and international communities.

9. Rather our responsibility may be to champion such communities, pinpoint the factors creating them, and take seriously their question-mark against our present society.

10. We are ill-served by our present spirituality for squaring up to conflict, for absorbing punishment without deference. We need training in affording those who are violent space and time to find positive channels for their aggressions.

The Profile of Love

'A timid, obscure gospel is no gospel at all.'
William Wilberforce

'The weight of the past was too oppressive for
more than a stabilized vitality.' (Previte-Orton)

Like the late Roman Empire, referred to in this quotation, the Church today continues to attract loyalty, that of the concerned, the responsible and the worried — the essential stabilizing forces in any society. Always at hand to prop up a deserving cause, these good people lend the Church such stabilized vitality as it still has.

The question is whether Christianity can ever be content to be a 'deserving cause' in this sense, a religious encrustation on the face of secularity. To pose the question is to dismiss it.

The Christian faith, as the Confessing Church in Germany once reminded us, is a permanent affront to the decent consensus of the ordinary man. Yahweh, the Avenger of blood, stands implacably on the frontier between good and evil. To smudge this distinction may be our greatest temptation today:

> 'We to whom sins are venial crimes write loose poems that drift in air like today's news.
> Our justice, mercy to misguided foes.'
> (Iain Crichton Smith)

Faith is the great divider as well as, and prior to being the great reconciler. To stand on the right

frontier at the right time is what confessing the
Faith means. What frontier should we be standing
on today?

How do we read the signs of the times aright?
How are we to know what the key issue for our day
is? For the primitive Church it was the question of
Jew and Gentile. For the Fathers Christology. For
the Cistercian monk self-abandonment. For Luther
the righteousness of faith. And for us?

Where do we being to search? With the Bible,
the empirical church, with Jesus, with tradition,
with our neighbour, with the voice within? To these
abstract questions there are only abstract answers.

Theoretically the decision is fraught with such difficulties that many have abandoned hope and re-
treated to the detached joys of the analyst:

> Of good and evil much they argued then,
> Of happiness and final misery,
> Passion and apathy and glory and shame:
> Vain wisdom all, and false philosophy!
> (Paradise Lost)

This disinclination to adopt dogmatic postures is
understandable. With our panoramic vision we can
see how often petty disputes have split Christendom, how seldom vision and reality have coincided
to let the great doors of transcendence spring open.
Few indeed were the issues which justified the sword
of division.

We need not be ashamed of the fact that we are,
in our pluralist society, hopeless exiles from the un-
conscious bigotries of the past. The sheared vision
remains an option only for those who consciously

144

opt for it. There are still those who would make a *casus confessionis* of eucharistic language or the shape of church government, or who feel the foundations toppling when drama displays nudes or uses dirty language. But such people, for all their illusions of a basically Christian society, inhabit sectarian tabernacles. They have, as is their good right and perhaps their need, of deliberation cut themselves off from the real world. They have no Gospel for it.

Only the sick need a doctor. Only the rough and tumble and tragedy of the secular arena needs the touch of transcendence. It was in the streets and fields, not the churches, that Francis of Assisi sang, in the artisans' workshops that Livingstone saw the Christian future of Africa, in the political quest for a new Germany that Bonhoeffer ran his last lap. It is the nightmare reality of an oppressed world which needs the dream of liberation, not the protected stockade of the Church. Our theology must be a responsive theology.

This is not to argue for the submergence of the Church in the world. Quite the opposite. Though the Church stockade is a misplaced boundary it is a distorted echo of a most proper concern. Without a clear profile of its own the Church is nothing at all. A theology hooked on relevance, parasitic on the chop and change of convention, is a monstrous perversion.

Liberation theology's stress on orthopraxis, on doing the truth, is helpful here. It is not a stockade of the right words which marks out the Church; it is right action. It is the proclamation of the Gospel by action.

In the autumn of 1976 a young East German pastor formulated this concern in six theses on 'proclamation by action':

1. My action is proclamation of the Gospel when I respond appropriately to the challenge of my situation; correct theology does not precede correct action; it is not its precondition; on the contrary, it comes at a later stage as one reflects on one's praxis.

2. In my situation proclamation of the Gospel is above all the attempt to raise people's consciousness.

3. Unjust social structures, which cause unrest and destroy life, constitute the first main challenge I have to face.

4. The second main challenge in my situation is the encounter with atheism, a component of the socialist ideology affirmed by me.

5. For the theological reflection on my action the prophetic message of the Old Testament, which involves judgement, penitence, and promise, is important.

6. That 'God became man' is the other decisive theological theme for me, indicating the ultimate seriousness of one's involvement in the struggle for more humanity.

This is the profile of the servant Church. It does not formulate programmes for others to carry out, in any case impossible in a Socialist state. Nor does it formulate programmes for itself based on the ideal principles of a timeless theology. It responds. It responds in its own way and from its own perspectives. This response is itself the Gospel it preaches. Only at a final stage is the response interrogated as to its theological presuppositions.

Similarly a theology of the just peace is a responsive theology. If we have eyes for seeing and ears for hearing, our will and imagination threaten to crumple under the well-documented examples of the oppression of the widow and orphan, the hungry and humiliated, the poor of the land. And if misery stalks the highways so do violence and fear and hate and war. None of this is news. Yet what else is offered us in our news bulletins than this non-news, the endless bulletins of misery, with a generous admixture of 'human interest' trivia.

Our response is 'good news': release to the captive, forgiveness to the ungodly, good news amidst the avalanche of bad news, of non-news. Ultimately good news to the oppressor as well, but in the first instance social and political dynamite. To know why Thomas Müntzer sided with the peasants in the social catastrophe which punctured the confidence of the Reformation one only has to read his version of the Beatitudes. No wonder the majority of church and state leaders soon came to the conclusion of Elizabeth of England that the Gospel was too explosive to be put in the hands of the common man, except in carefully doctored form.

History, 'the long, difficult, confused dream of humanity' (Schopenhauer) reminds us of this heroic dimension of the Faith, of the saint-studded past of the Church, a deadly embarrassment to us moderns, pygmies indeed on the shoulders of giants. For what characterises British Church and society today is the great stampede for the middle ground, the universalisation of the insurance mentality, taking thought for every conceivable tomorrow, keeping all options open and no guns firing.

147

Those committed by the gratuity of the Gospel are committed to risk, not to the middle road. The just peace is not a programme. It is an impossible dream. To live for and by this dream is to inhabit the Christian reality, to be midwives of miracles, of the new birth which alone makes the struggle meaningful. Martin Luther King's dream of freedom will never come to pass, yet unless we wager our life on it what is life worth, what does it mean?

The Gospel which makes an insider of the outsider commits him or her simultaneously to those without the walls, to the atheist, the down-trodden, the outcast. Those for whom all walls of partition have been torn down cannot blithely erect new ones of their own making. For the Christian the only safe way is the perilous one; living for the impossible tomorrow, interlacing the prose of actuality with the rhythm of hope, calling defiance to Satan as he squats like a cormorant on the Tree of Life.

We could do, perhaps, with something of the defiant triumphalism of the Counter-Reformation. In Baroque churches the Ecce Homo is often crowned with a blazing golden aureole. The way of suffering, the way of the Cross, is thus pronounced the triumphant one, shattering the foundations of the old cosmos, bringing in the new.

But to pronounce oneself on the side of love — even all-conquering love — is to ensure that unanimity of support which betokens total incomprehension. This is one of the advantages of the term 'liberation', abused and misunderstood as it has been. To say, 'all we need is liberation' comes less trippingly off the tongue than 'all we need is love', no doubt because the commitment to liberation is a commitment to change. Our sentimentalised notion of love tends to hide this. To say, 'I love you', without the 'I' being at least in part a strong, Christlike 'I am', is simply to express one's own need.

In the end of the day, though, the words chosen do not matter all that much; liberation or love, righteousness or peace. In the Old Testament as in the New, terms like righteousness and peace tend to come in couplets or triplets or more. They are inseparable. Slogans are, in any case, only as credible as their bearers.

Let us abide, then, by the term 'love'. Let us risk misunderstanding and say that the primary contribution of the Church in the field of peace and justice is to allow this profile of love to emerge. So often Church pronouncements seem to fall 'betwixt twa stules', hobbling uneasily between realism and idealism, addressed to a non-existent Christian consensus, a no-man's-land between state and church. As a result they can appear to underestimate the intractability of the issues, on the one hand, and the originality of the Gospel perspective on the other. They end up by offering good advice (often genuinely good advice) to the 'others' who have to carry it out — to the politicians, the social planners, the men of affairs.

Perhaps we have to stop offering 'others' good advice. Perhaps we ourselves have to become these 'others'. For the umpire role is as much a delusion for us as it became for the popes of the Middle Ages. Our role, rather, should be a responsive one.

A theology of the just peace responds to the injustice and violence in us and around us. To the ex-

tent that it is genuine response and not mere reaction it introduces a new element into the situation, gives others pause for thought and room for
manoeuvre. If, as so often, we fail to do more than
react, we can be forbearing enough with ourselves to
ask why, to learn from our verbal or actual violence,
our panic or impatience or touchiness. Even a failed
response, perhaps it most of all, is a cause for
gratitude, a laboratory for learning. The withdrawal
from any response at all, in the anxiety lest mistakes
be made, is the greatest temptation of all. Blessed
are they who respond, for they may do better next
time...

Our response, too, need not always be a
measured, emotion-free one. Is anger always weakness? Is it wrong to boil with rage at the humiliation
and hurt of the child or the alcoholic or the
wounded self? Unless we rage at injustice we are
diminished in our humanity. Without a touch of
aggression there is no true compassion. "How long,
O Lord?" It may be significant that in the Psalms,
for example, so much of the real rage is directed at
God himself.

Cool detachment is a false ideal. Who are we to
play God, looking with an infinite fund of compassion at those who cheapen life and strip away the
shreds of dignity? We have to take sides. To
imagine that our spiritual vantage-point puts us
above the contending parties is either arrogance or
self-delusion.

But in what action, by what gesture do we allow
the profile of love to emerge? How do we ensure
that we are responding and not just reacting? How
do we step out of the vicious circle of alienation and

enable others to do the same? How can our actions anticipate the Kingdom, document the dream?

Sobriety is in place here. Our ability to do anything at all may be extremely limited. We may be the wrong people for it. And some situations are, in human terms, hopeless. Alighting from a helter-skelter in mid-air tends to be inadvisable. The arms race or class conflict or the tensions at home or in the office so often seem to have this helter-skelter quality, joyrides gone irremediably sour.

Yet the attempt has to be made. 'Unless we can make friends of our enemies, we will soon make enemies of our friends.' Again and again this study has stressed the need to face the reality of conflict, that whatever our ultimate faith in the goodness of creation, in Christ, in our neighbour, in lions lying down with lambs, there can be no evasion of our penultimate duty: to lay bare the anatomy of conflict, to see the divisive issues straight, to lay the cards on the table, to spell things out.

Justice demands this. Far from resolving the conflict this may, of course, even trigger off violence. But being a door-mat is no part of the Christian vocation, still less making door-mats of others, in however subtle a way. So the distrust, anxiety, hatred, simply has to be faced, without resort to self-pity or explosions of wrath, both of which, of course, simply confirm the other in the belief that his hostility is amply justified.

It is a tall order. The merest hair-line separates firmness and obduracy, flexibility and weakness. To some extent training in group discipline can sharpen one's perception of these frontiers. The benevolently ruthless group may well be the best educator for the

151

would-be reconciler. It is not, however, a matter of learning non-violent 'techniques'. All good relationships are sheer miracle, forged in the face of incredible odds. Simplistic talk of techniques merits the most sceptical scrutiny. Miracles — and that is the business we are in — can never be engineered.

If persuasion fails, what then? Do we use coercion to bring about justice? (Is there any justice without law, any law without coercion?) Do we defend the weak and the victimised, if necessary, with the gun? If we have the power to stop naked aggression have we any choice but to use it?

These are not rhetorical questions. No doubt, as the young East German pastor suggests, action cannot be theologically determined or legitimated in advance. We would do well, however, to examine whether such apparently altruistic actions are not rooted in self-interest, and to ask, too, whether what is appropriate for the secular state is also appropriate to the Church.

The same queries would apply if actual fighting broke out: What does the Christian do then? Pray for victory or pray for peace? Condemn, abstain from, participate in, or seek to limit the hostilities? Prepare to pick up such pieces as are left when the slaughter is over?

In the course of our two years of discussions we reviewed many violent situations. We found very few in which, even from a purely rational analysis, violence seemed a possible way to tackle injustice. For me personally, the risk and the sickening challenge and the real hope all seem to lie in the non-violent alternative. How can one rescue dignity and humanity by the gun?

This, again, is not a 'rhetorical question'. How can we fail to feel with those who, in their quest for justice, have encountered only the iron hand of repression, and have been driven in desperation to violence themselves? If we would stand on this frontier of the future, if we believe that it is here, in the struggle for justice, that the Christian today must stand up and be counted, if the profile of love is not to be sentimentalised out of recognition, we will need hard heads as well as gentle hearts, we will have to produce the more convincing analysis, the better alternatives, the costlier discipleship.

The immensity of the challenge is daunting. It is so clearly 'beyond us'. But if, as we believe, the way of the Cross has the future on its side, then even in our confused present we can be fired with a perverse confidence, a defiant gaiety, and the vision of peace and justice may be anticipated in some small measure by the profile of our love.

Working Party

Edinburgh Group

Chairman: Steven Mackie, Chairman of International Sub-committee of Church and Nation Committee of the Church of Scotland; lecturer in Practical Theology, University of St. Andrews; wide experience in ecumenical affairs and the Third World.

Members: Ronald Beasley. President of International Fellowship of Reconciliation, adviser to Convent of the Good Shepherd, Edinburgh on residential Social work; has pioneered many projects in voluntary youth and community work.

Peter Birrell. Young Church of Scotland minister; particular interest in life-style questions.

Geoffrey Carnall. Reader in English literature, Edinburgh University; experience in India, Northern Ireland; Quaker.

Hugh Davidson. Minister of Church of Scotland in rural and urban parishes; concerned with world development.

Marcus Lefebure. Roman Catholic Chaplain, University of Edinburgh; Dominican.

Kay Little. Housewife, mother of two; lived during project in Easterhouse, deprived housing estate in Glasgow.

Edwin Lucas. Retired civil servant; elder of Church of Scotland; honorary treasurer of project.

Robert Murphy. Young Roman Catholic priest; interest in liberation theology.

Andrew Ross. Dean of Faculty of Divinity and Principal of New College, Edinburgh; ex‑missionary in Malawi; church historian.

Elizabeth Templeton. Lecturer in theology; interest in Christian-Marxist dialogue.

Alastair Weir. New Testament lecturer, St. Andrews University; ex-missionary in Zaire and Dean of Theology Faculty there.

London Group

Chairman: David Mumford. Anglican layman, worked with Christian Aid, Cyrenians, now with the National Association for Mental Health.

Alex Cosgrave. Journalist on the *Catholic Herald*, formerly on youth staff of Fellowship of Reconciliation.

Roy Earnshaw. Businessman, with particular interest in industrial relations.

Bruce Kent. Chaplain to *Pax Christi*; was Roman Catholic chaplain University of London.

Alan Kreider. Warden of London Mennonite Centre; concerned with experiments in communal life.

Andrew Morton. Social Responsibility Secretary of the British Council of Churches; experience as parish minister in Scotland and chaplain to Edinburgh University.

Belfast Group

The members of this group must remain anonymous. It would cripple or at least restrict their present work if their views, as frankly expressed here, were made public. Some indication of the composition of the group may, however, be found helpful.

About half the members are Protestants (nearly all Presbyterians), half Roman Catholic. They include a prominent Church leader, a married couple living in one of the areas of Belfast worst hit by the troubles, two Presbyterian ministers from 'hard-line' Protestant districts, two Roman Catholic clergymen, and a couple involved in the mixed marriage situation.